DON'T PANIC!

A Teen's Guide to Managing Social Anxiety

With CBT-based Challenges & Exercises

AYA WANG

Chapters

Chapter 1 "Why Do I Feel This Way?"
"All you need to know about Social Anxiety Disorder,
but in a fun way!"

Meet Isa & Jeremy—What is Social Anxiety?—What are its causes, myths, triggers and symptoms?—What are avoidance and safety behaviors?—How does Social Anxiety work?

Chapter 2: "Reprogram Your Brain"
"CBT- based techniques to rewire your brain and manage
negative thoughts."

Do you believe that your brain has superpowers?—Learn how your brain works and how to stop letting it trick you—Master the steps for defeating negative thinking patterns.

Chapter 3: "Calm Your Body"
"Effective coping strategies to soothe your body when anxious."

Discover how you can use your body to reduce social anxiety—Upskill yourself in breathing, grounding, visualization, progressive muscle relaxation techniques—Familiarize yourself with the panic attack cheat sheet to calm yourself when they happen.

Chapter 4: "Embrace The Suck"
"Steps to gradually face your fears head-on using Exposure Therapy"

How avoidance fuels the cycle of anxiety—Why embracing the suck is the most powerful way of getting over social anxiety—How you can slowly and gradually face your fears without overwhelming yourself.

Chapter 5: "The Significant Six"
"Six science-backed habits that will help you keep your anxiety under control."

Discover how habits can fuel or reduce your anxiety—Learn about the power of getting quality sleep, eating right, moving your body, spreading kindness, journaling and mindfulness.

Chapter 6: "Your Quest For Support"
"Strategies for talking about your social anxiety and seeking help"

Why you should talk about what you're dealing with and how to go about it—Identify your roadblocks and learn how to challenge them—When is it time to consider therapy?—Reframing therapy—How therapy can make all the difference

The End Game

Useful Resources

References

Content

CHAPTER 1

Why Do I Feel This Way?

Meet Isa

Isa glanced through the kitchen window as her little brother Noah tried (and failed) to dunk a basketball in the driveway.

Isa snickered. Noah might have been more popular than Isa, but he had nothing on her when it came to skills on the court. Laughing, she turned from the window to open the fridge. But just as her fingers wrapped around the refrigerator handle, she caught a glimpse of something that stopped her cold.

Amid the jumble of photos, flyers, and scribbled notes decorated the refrigerator door, Isa saw something new. It was something that she hoped would never come—something she'd been dreading for weeks.

Printed on bright orange paper and posted under a little square magnet was a letter from Northland High School.

Dear Parents and Students,

As the new school year approaches, we'd like to extend a warm welcome to all of our incoming 9th-grade students. We look forward to seeing your child for 9th-grade Orientation Day on Wednesday, August 17, from 8:00 AM – 3:00 PM in the auditorium...

Isa couldn't bring herself to read the rest of the letter. She glanced at the calendar beside the refrigerator and groaned. It was already Monday, and that meant she had less than 48 hours before officially starting high school.

Her mouth suddenly felt like sandpaper.

Thick, heavy dread sank into her heart like an anchor dropping to the bottom of a lake. Her stomach did somersaults, and she thought her heart might pound right out of her chest. She wiped her hands, suddenly dripping with sweat, against the fabric of her shorts.

Without the daily pressure of socializing with classmates, Isa felt like a bird that had been released from its cage. No more awkward small talk to endure, no more fake smiles to plaster on her face, and no more feeling like a fish out of water.

She didn't have to answer questions while the entire class stared, their eyes boring into her as though she was on trial. Nor did she have to endure the agony of giving a speech in front of the class while stumbling over her words, or the triple agony of hearing her mother nag about why she wasn't going to 8th-grade Formal.

Her anxious thoughts filled her mind

She was starting 9th grade at the high school, which had four times the amount of people as her middle school. And since Isa would have to deal with them every day for the next four years, she landed on the idea that high school would be at least sixteen times as horrible as middle school. The numbers were terrifying:

452 middle school kids x

4

1,808 kids x

4 years

7,232 reasons to hate high school

Isa's anxiety was like a virus, infecting every thought and feeling she had about starting high school. Not only would she have to navigate the academic challenges, but she'd also have to dodge fourteen different formals and dances over the next four years.

Isa's stomach churned like a washing machine on high speed, and she bolted towards the bathroom, hoping to make it before the contents of her breakfast made a reappearance.

Meet Jeremy

"If you're not down here in five minutes, we're leaving without you," Jeremy's father called sternly from the living room.

Fine with me, Jeremy thought, smugly.

With only two more days of freedom left before he had to start the 10th grade, Jeremy wished everyone would just leave him be. But his parents insisted on dragging him to Ashton Levine's birthday party, and no amount of pleading or feigning a mysterious headache, stomachache, every-part-of-his-body-ache could get him out of it this time.

As Jeremy laced up his sneakers, he mentally rehearsed his lines for the impending encounter with Ashton and the rest of the party-goers.

Truth be told, Jeremy didn't consider Ashton to be a friend in the first place.

Sure, they may have been classmates since the 3rd grade and their parents may have been inseparable but, in Jeremy's mind, Ashton was nothing more than an acquaintance. Jeremy admired Ashton's quick wit and effortless charm from afar, but always felt tongue-tied whenever their parents insisted that they hang out together.

Jeremy descended the stairs with a sense of unease gnawing at his gut. He had rehearsed his lines for the party a thousand times, but the thought of being caught off guard still sent shivers down his spine.

What if Ashton's friends asked him something he hadn't planned for? What if they saw through his facade of confidence and realized he was just a socially awkward mess?

Jeremy tried to shake off the anxiety and put on a brave face but, deep down, he knew that tonight could make or break his social standing.

"Come on, buddy," his father said, squeezing Jeremy's shoulder as they headed to the car.

"The birthday party will be a blast," Jeremy's mother chimed in. "It was so nice of Ashton to invite you. It's good for you to socialize a bit before school starts."

"I don't even talk to Ashton and those guys," Jeremy said, clicking his seatbelt.

"Just don't let your shyness get the best of you. It's about time you started to grow out of this phase," his mother said brightly.

Easy for you to say, Jeremy thought.

Jeremy spent the rest of the car ride thinking back over the conversations he'd rehearsed in his mind.

But, once his parents dropped him off, nothing went as planned.

As Jeremy stood in the driveway, Ashton came out to greet him and headed in for a high five.

"Hey, Jeremy. How's your summer?" Ashton said.

Ashton's outstretched hand hung awkwardly in the air like a lonely flag flapping in the wind. Jeremy's mind went blank, and he felt like a computer that suddenly crashed. He wished he could press Ctrl+Alt+Delete and restart the conversation. But instead, Jeremy stood there, frozen with anxiety, and unable to form a coherent sentence.

"It's—well, I've been—uh," Jeremy stuttered, his face flushing bright red.

The silence grew heavier, suffocating Jeremy. It was as if all the words he had so carefully rehearsed had escaped his mind, leaving him stranded in an uncomfortable limbo. He could feel Ashton's eyes boring into him, waiting for a response. But his mind was blank.

As Jeremy's hands continued to tremble, he couldn't help but feel as though he was unraveling in front of Ashton. His stomach churned, and his heart pounded so loudly in his chest that he was sure Ashton could hear it. Jeremy knew he had to say something, anything, to break the silence.

But his tongue felt like it was glued to the roof of his mouth, and he couldn't force a single word out.

"Alright, man," Ashton interjected at long last. "Want to head inside with the other guys? We're just about to play a game."

Jeremy nodded, silently praying that the game was Hide and Seek, so he could curl up into a corner and disappear until the party ended.

What's Going On With Isa and Jeremy?

You can likely relate to how Isa felt—summer break is like a sweet escape to a far-off land with endless possibilities. But as the first day of school approaches, that vacation high comes crashing down like a sandcastle in a hurricane. Suddenly, the mere thought of returning to the classroom is enough to send shivers down your spine and make your stomach churn like a blender.

And then there's the pre-social event jitters. For most people, it's just a few butterflies flapping around inside, but for Jeremy, it's like a swarm of angry bees, ready to sting him if he makes one wrong move.

So why do those teenagers feel this way?

Imagine the caveman days when giant mammals lived among humans. Huge bears, monster crocodiles, and ferocious sabretooth tigers roamed the Earth. Whenever they interacted with humans, they mostly tried to eat us.

With so much danger everywhere, our human ancestors did something fascinating to help the species survive. They developed a "fight, flight, or freeze" mechanism in the part of their brains called the amygdala. This mechanism gave their bodies a shot of adrenaline whenever they were in danger so they could fly like the wind to safety or put up the fight of their lives against predators.

Even though we don't have to battle beasts anymore, this survival mechanism continues to exist in our brains to this day. That's why when we think we're in danger, our bodies react as if we're being chased by T-Rexes and Dilophosauruses (the quick little guys with the weird neck frills that can run really fast).

So when Isa saw the notice about 9th-grade Orientation on the fridge, her brain may as well have thought she was being charged by a pack of hungry hyenas. And when Ashton started making small talk, Jeremy's amygdala said, "Ahh! We're being attacked!"

But why?

Isa and Jeremy have something in common—they both have **social anxiety disorder (SAD).**

SAD is defined as experiencing terror, hyper-self-consciousness, and strong physical arousal in social situations over and over again. It's like having an unwanted and uninvited guest crashing a party in your brain every time you socialize.

Social anxiety is different from everyday anxiety. The feeling you get when you're about to take a test or when you're nervous about meeting new people—that "butterflies in your stomach" feeling— is perfectly normal.

But social anxiety is when that feeling doesn't go away or gets so bad that it interferes with your everyday life. It's an intense, crippling fear of social situations that makes your body react like it's being chased by a starving bear.

People with social anxiety might avoid going to school, or they might not want to leave the house at all. Making and keeping friends can be tricky, and dates are out of the question. Even talking on the phone or ordering food at a restaurant can be difficult.

That Sounds Like Being Shy—Are They the Same Thing?

Let's face it, we all feel a little shy sometimes.

It's normal to feel unsure and uneasy in social situations that are new or important to us. Whether it's the first day of school, a class presentation, or meeting someone for the first time, those butterflies in our stomachs can make us clam up into our shells. Shyness is often characterized by a passive or quiet manner, and it's a common experience for many people. However, it doesn't turn into intense fear and crippling physical symptoms.

Social anxiety, on the other hand, is different. It's more than just being shy. It's an ongoing fear of social situations, often leading to avoidance behavior and causing a lot of distress. This fear can be so intense that it triggers physical symptoms such as rapid heartbeat, sweating, trembling, shortness of breath and nausea (just to name a few). It can affect various areas of a person's life, from school and work to personal relationships and daily activities.

Sound familiar?

Here's a not-so-secret secret—you're not the only one who feels this way. *Millions* of people live with SAD.

But there's a lot of misinformation about social anxiety floating around in the world. And when you don't have all the facts, it can make living with SAD even harder.

So let's see if you can spot some common social anxiety myths!

Challenge: Spot the Myths

- Social anxiety is a freak occurrence that happens randomly.

- The thoughts that cause social anxiety are uncontrollable.

- If you're an introvert, then you have social anxiety.

- Extroverts don't get social anxiety.

- People with social anxiety feel anxious all the time.

- People only feel social anxiety when they're around strangers or people they aren't close to.

- Social anxiety is uncomfortable, but it's mostly harmless.

- Eventually, people will grow out of social anxiety and get over it.

- You can only cure social anxiety with medication.

- Once your brain is wired to think a certain way, you can't teach it how to manage anxious thoughts.

- Socially anxious people don't want friends—they're fine being alone most of the time.

Ready to check your answers?

Well, this will be fast—they're all myths! That's right. Every single one is a common myth about social anxiety. Here's the truth about each of the myths above:

Correcting Common Myths About SAD:

- SAD can be caused by genetics and early social development experiences.

- You can control anxious thoughts with research-based techniques.

- Introverts don't necessarily have social anxiety. Introverted people simply feel energetically recharged when they spend quality time by themselves.

- Extroverts can experience social anxiety like everyone else, including celebrities who appear totally confident on TV.

- People with SAD can feel relaxed when they're in a comfortable environment. But, there are unique triggers that cause symptoms of SAD.

- SAD can flare up around friends and loved ones, too. In fact, you may know someone suffering from SAD who doesn't let it show. It's not always visible!

- Social anxiety can hinder you from achieving your dreams if left unchecked.

- Cognitive-behavioral therapy (CBT) and mindfulness techniques are essential parts of managing SAD.

- Medication is a treatment for SAD, but it's not the only option.

- You can rewire your brain to better manage the symptoms of SAD.

- It's not true that socially anxious people don't want friends. They just struggle with socializing to the point that it becomes too much of a hassle. In the end, they deal with one of the most burdensome symptoms of social anxiety: loneliness.

Is Social Anxiety Disorder Uncommon?

Like many people with Social Anxiety Disorder (SAD), Isa and Jeremy think they're freaks, as if they're the only ones in the world who feel this way.

But they're wrong!

Social anxiety is so common that there are researchers who dedicate their lives to studying it. In fact, it's estimated that about 2%-5% of the world population experience SAD. That's as many as *400 million people*.

No matter what continent you live on, which country you grow up in, or what your identity is, there are people just like you who live with symptoms of SAD every single day.

Here are some quick stats:

- Social anxiety disorder is the world's third most common mental health condition.

- Women and men are equally likely to seek treatment for social anxiety, though one study found that women are slightly more likely to have the condition.

- You're probably more likely to experience social anxiety if you live in countries like America, China, Brazil, and India. Interestingly, these are also countries with some of the largest populations.

- Most studies have found that social anxiety starts in adolescence.

Why Do Teens Like Isa & Jeremy Have SAD, But Teens Like Ashton & Noah Don't?

Social anxiety is like a ninja ambush, silently creeping up on you when you least expect it. It's not caused by walking under a ladder, passing by a broken mirror or crossing paths with a black cat. So don't blame your misfortunes on superstitions—social anxiety is a whole other beast.

Here are a few things that may increase your risk:

Genetics
Research shows that certain genes can increase your chances of developing social anxiety disorder, so if it runs in your family, you might want to keep an eye out for any symptoms. It's like playing a genetic lottery, but instead of winning a million dollars, you might end up with a predisposition for social anxiety.

Puberty
Puberty can be a tricky time, and it's not just because of the awkward growth spurts and acne. Teens undergo a mind-blowing transformation during this phase of life. Picture this: you're like a sculptor molding a masterpiece, shaping your personality, and witnessing your own body's growth and development. It's a time of vulnerability, where the winds of change blow strong. While you're on this journey, it's no surprise that SAD can rear its ugly head.

Environment
Your environment can also play a significant role in whether you develop social anxiety. Childhood trauma, isolation, overprotective parents, and bullying are all factors that can increase your risk of experiencing SAD in the future.

Brain Chemistry
Scientists have found that people with social anxiety have a particular brain chemistry compared to those without the condition. It's like having

a brain that's wired a little differently, like a circuit board that's been assembled with some extra wires or components. For example, your brain might produce more of the stress hormone cortisol, or have different levels of neurotransmitters, which are like chemical messengers that transmit signals between brain cells.

Doesn't SAD Eventually Go Away on its Own?
Social anxiety disorder *can* get better for some teens as they get older. But for a lot of people it doesn't go away without some self-help intervention or professional treatment.

So, there's a chance that it could disappear on its own?

There is a chance, yes, but you don't want to take that risk because the possible consequences are *NOT* fun. Unfortunately, the aftermath of social anxiety left unchecked shows no mercy.

Left untreated, SAD can lead to:

- Low self-esteem
- Negative self-talk
- Poor social skills
- Isolation
- Dysfunctional relationships
- Substance abuse
- Low academic and professional achievement
- Depression
- Suicidal thoughts

Okay, you get it. If you think you may have some symptoms of social anxiety, this book will help you to find out more.

You may discover as you read on, that your feelings are caused by something else. But whether you have it or not, SAD is *not* something you should ignore.

Information is power, so let's continue this quest to discover what those teenage anxieties are all about, and how you can feel better about yourself if you are dealing with SAD.

High five!

Does Social Anxiety Feel the Same for Everyone?

Let's think back to Jeremy and Isa's story at the beginning of the chapter. Maybe their stories felt familiar—a little *too* familiar. When your brain perceives a threat (like an uncomfortable social situation), it sends signals to your body to guard against danger, causing you to feel, act, and think in ways you usually wouldn't.

People can experience social anxiety differently.

For Isa, social anxiety makes her feel an overwhelming sense of dread and fear. She becomes sweaty and nauseated as her heart pounds out of her chest and her face turns red. For Jeremy, his social anxiety causes him to clam up, shake uncontrollably, and forget everything he wants to say.

Social anxiety can show itself in many different ways, like a chameleon changing its colors. For some, it's like being on a rollercoaster with your stomach in your throat. For others, it's like being trapped in a haunted house with no way out. No matter the form it takes, social anxiety can feel like a weight on your chest that's impossible to shake off.

You're a complex, unique person. If you have SAD, it can look and feel differently from others, but there are a few commonalities among people who experience it.

SAD can feel like this:

- Self-consciousness in everyday situations like talking to peers, going to the store, making a phone call, or getting your hair cut.

- Intense stress before going to a social event.

- Extreme fear of being watched or judged by others.

- Anxious that you'll humiliate yourself in front of others.

- Fear that others will notice you're nervous.

SAD can look like this:

- Blushing
- Butterflies or nausea
- Shaking voice and body
- Racing heart
- Sweating or hot flashes
- Foggy brain
- Blackouts

- Shortness of breath
- Shaking voice and body
- Tightness in your chest
- Feeling dizzy
- Panic or anxiety attacks
- Muscle stiffness

SAD can make you act like this:

- Going to extremes to avoid social situations.

- Hiding in the background.

- Staying quiet even when you have a strong opinion.

- You need to bring a friend wherever you go.

- Drinking alcohol or abusing substances in social situations to soothe your nerves.

- Not introducing yourself to new people.

- Avoiding eye contact.

- Spending most of the day at home or alone.

- Not able to be stand up for yourself or be assertive.

- Using distractions when you're around people.

Self-Assessment: Do I Have Social Anxiety?

Are you reading this book because you think you might have social anxiety?

This self-assessment provides scenarios to help you determine if you might be dealing with a social anxiety disorder. Assess your level of anxiety in each situation using this scale:

Self-Assessment:
Could I have Social Anxiety?

Smooth Sailing (No Anxiety) 1	Don't Love It (Some Anxiety) 2	Hate It (More Anxiety) 3	NOPE NOPE NOPE (High Anxiety) 4

1.___Introducing yourself in front of the class.

2.___Greeting someone you don't know.

3.___Coming up with something to say during an awkward silence.

4.___Correcting someone during a conversation.

5.___Answering a question in front of the whole class.

6.___Being the last one to enter a full classroom.

7.___Getting a phone call from someone you don't know.

8.___Tripping over your shoelaces in the school cafeteria.

9.___Taking a walk by yourself.

10.___Asking a classmate to quiet down so you can focus on your work.

11.___Asking someone new to go on a date with you.

12.___Reading a paragraph out loud to the class.

13.___Shopping for new clothes at the mall by yourself.

14.___Asking a worker if they have something in your size.

15.___Working on a group project with other students you don't know.

16.___Giving someone feedback on something they created.

17.___Standing up for yourself to a bully.

18.___ Eating in a crowded cafeteria.

19.___ Asking someone if the seat next to them is free.

20.___ Inviting a classmate to hang out after school.

Now add your scores.

If your total score is 30 or higher, you might have social anxiety – but don't panic! That's why we're here in the first place.

This is not a diagnosis of your anxiety, and it's not intended to be a substitute for medical advice. This is for informational purposes only. These are common signs of social anxiety.

But I Don't Always Feel That Way, So What Gives?

Social anxiety doesn't mean you always feel panicked like you're trying to outrun a Sabretooth Tiger. When you're hanging out with someone you feel comfortable around, you might be entirely at ease. Instead, social anxiety is triggered by specific things that might happen throughout your day.

Triggers are changes in the surroundings that affect your senses and heighten your social anxiety. For example, attending a crowded party, giving a speech, or making small talk with a stranger might be triggers that make you feel anxious.

Common Examples of Triggers:

- Public speaking, performing on stage, being called on in class, being watched, or being the center of attention.

- Being teased, criticized, or bullied in school.

- Talking to a cashier or worker.

- Eating or drinking in public, using public restrooms, going shopping, or doing anything else where you might run into other people.

- Making phone calls, attending parties, or other activities that require you to interact with other people.

Even Isa and Jeremy have their own special triggers.

Isa was minding her own business, having a perfectly normal day playing basketball with her brother until she realized she had a big school orientation on the horizon. Cue her social anxiety, which turns her into a sweaty, heart-pounding mess when faced with large crowds or socializing in school.

Once Jeremy learned he had to go to a classmate's birthday bash, he instantly felt his social anxiety start to stir. He dreads small group gatherings because he's terrified of making small talk and possibly coming off as a bumbling fool.

Social anxiety triggers look different for everyone, so if your self-assessment shows that you probably have SAD, knowing your triggers is one of the first steps toward taking back control of how your brain responds to social situations.

Challenge: List Your Anxiety Triggers

We're all unique individuals, and our triggers can vary.

For example:

- Ordering food in a restaurant and mispronouncing a word on the menu.
- Getting up to leave for the restroom in the middle of class while everyone stares at me.
- Underdressing or overdressing for a party with people I don't know.

List as many as you can think of. Take your time!

_____

_____

_____

_____

Isa's First Day of School

Isa's alarm clock screeched like a banshee at 6:30 AM on Wednesday morning. But Isa was wide awake; she had spent the last two nights tossing and turning like a ship in a stormy sea. She laid in bed, racking her brain for any conceivable excuse to skip 9th-grade Orientation.

However, deep down, Isa knew her mother would never fall for it. Just like a bloodhound on the scent, her mother could sniff out a fake excuse from a mile away. So, Isa begrudgingly crawled out of bed and prepared to face her dreaded first day of high school.

As she brushed her teeth, Isa began looking hard at her reflection. A few pimples had erupted over the last couple of days, and bags had started to form under her eyes from lack of sleep.

Isa had always avoided makeup, feeling as though it would only draw attention to her and make her *more* self-conscious. But today was different. Today was the first day of high school, and she was determined to make a good impression.

So she did something she'd never done before—Isa nervously sat down in front of her mother's vanity mirror, her palms already clammy. She tentatively picked up a tube of foundation, carefully applying it to her face. As she moved on to blush and mascara, she started to feel a sense of pride and accomplishment. With every layer of makeup, she felt like she was donning a disguise, hoping to blend in with the rest of the world.

Maybe this was what it felt like to be confident?

When she was done, Isa stared at her reflection with a mix of horror and fascination, feeling like a mad scientist. But would anyone notice the real Isa beneath the mask of concealer and foundation?

Suddenly, her little brother Noah barged into the room, barely knocking before entering and yelling, "Mom says she's about to leave without you!"

He took one look at Isa and burst into laughter.

"What are you doing?" he chortled. "You look like a clown!"

"You wouldn't know beauty if it slapped you in the face," Isa quipped back as her face flushed red with embarrassment.

Did I overdo it? Do I really look like a clown?

"Isa, you have thirty seconds to get your butt down here," her mother called.

There was no time to go back now.

After her mother dropped her off in the carpool line, Isa stood frozen for several minutes. A long line of students snaked around the school building, all of them waiting to pick up their new schedules. Reluctantly, she trudged her way to the rear of the line.

A tall girl standing in front of her with a long, dark ponytail turned and smiled.

"Isn't this exciting? I can't wait to see who my teachers are. I hear Mr. Burkey is pretty nice. But I don't want Mrs. Stark—my sister says she's mean as an alligator with a toothache."

Isa raised her eyebrows, nodded her head, and forced a smile.

"I'm Marcy," the girl went on. "Nice to meet you. What's your name?"

Isa gulped and whispered in a barely audible tone, "Hi, I'm Isa."

"Did you say Lisa? You're a real quiet talker, Lisa!"

Isa didn't bother to correct her.

Jeremy's Birthday Party Disaster

Jeremy stared up at his ceiling the night after the birthday party. He mentally replayed the events of Ashton's birthday party like a broken record. It was like his brain was stuck in a never-ending loop of cringe-worthy moments.

He remembered walking into the house with Ashton, where a group of guys from school sat around snacking on chips, laughing, and talking. Jeremy felt like all eyes were on him, and his heart began racing. He tried to act naturally, as if he belonged there, but his awkwardness seemed to radiate off him like a neon sign.

"Hey everyone, this is Jeremy. You've probably seen him around school," Ashton said, as he introduced his friend.

One of the boys at the party nodded and said, "Hey man, what's up?"

Jeremy's mind went blank, and he could feel his face turning red. He opened his mouth to say something, anything, but all that came out was a pathetic "uhhh ... sup?"

It was like his social skills had been sucked out of him, leaving only a gaping void of embarrassment.

That wasn't even the worst of it. Jeremy pulled the covers over his face as he remembered what happened next.

After they all sang "Happy Birthday" and finished cake and ice cream, they decided to play Two Truths and a Lie. Everyone came up with what they wanted to say so fast, but by the time they got to Jeremy, all he could manage was, "anyone need more soda?"

Just then, there was a knock at the door.

"Jeremy," Ashton said, "you mind grabbing that since you're up?"

He knew this couldn't be good. When Jeremy opened the door, he was horrified to see three girls he recognized from school.

Jeremy nodded, trying to find his voice. The girl who spoke first, a very pretty girl with long, strawberry-blonde hair, flashed him a smile and introduced herself.

"Hi, I'm Shania. We're here for Ashton's party."

Jeremy's mind went blank.

"We're sorry we're late," she continued. "We got a little lost on the way here. Do you mind if we come in?"

Jeremy said nothing. He moved out of the way, allowing the girls to enter. As they passed him, he could hear them whispering and giggling to each other, and he felt his face burn with embarrassment.

"I'm sorry, Ashton," Jeremy whispered quietly when he came back inside. "I'm not feeling so great—bad stomachache. So I think I'm gonna head home."

"You sure, man? It's the last day of summer break, you sure you want to spend it at home?"

Jeremy felt a knot form in his stomach as he remembered Ashton's quizzical expression. He couldn't shake the feeling that Ashton had seen right through his flimsy excuse.

But the feeling of relief Jeremy felt when he finally got home was *so sweet.*

He let out a frustrated sigh and rolled over onto his side. Why did social situations have to be so difficult? It felt like everyone else had it all figured out while he stumbled around like a clueless fool.

Tomorrow, he'd have to face Ashton and the guys on their first day of school. He just had to find a way out of it.

Why Does SAD Make Me Do Awkward Things?

When it comes to socializing, your brain can be a bit of a drama queen. It's always on the lookout for potential embarrassment and emotional turmoil, and will stop at nothing to keep you safe. Enter **safety behaviors**—those little habits that your brain makes you do both consciously and unconsciously to save you from awkward moments at social gatherings.

Safety behaviors can look like:

- Asking the other person too many questions about themselves to avoid your turn to talk.

- Sitting in the corner or the back of the room to not get attention.

- Avoiding eye contact when speaking with someone.

- Offering to serve drinks, take pictures, or any other role that allows you to avoid socializing for too long.

- Drinking alcohol or taking drugs to feel less anxious.

- Mentally rehearsing (obsessively) what you'll say in conversations before they happen.

- Wearing too much makeup, clothing, and accessories that cover your body and face to avoid being seen, like hoodies, sunglasses, etc.

- Pretending to be sick to leave or avoid attending a social event.

- Constantly looking down at your phone or putting earphones in, to avoid being approached.

What Are Your Safety Behaviors?

When faced with a nerve-wracking social situation, it can be helpful to identify your go-to safety behaviors. Consider asking yourself these questions to start brainstorming some of your own tactics to avoid any chance of being embarrassed or anxious:

1. *How does your body language change when you can't get out of a social situation?*
2. *What are some things you do to avoid attention from other people?*
3. *Are there situations you've been in dozens of times that still make you anxious? How do you reduce your anxiety in those moments?*

Challenge: Identify Your Safety Behaviors

In the chart below, there are some examples of behaviors, and this challenge asks you to write down your own go-to safety behavior. After that, explain what you are trying to avoid when you use each behavior.

Safety Behavior	What are you trying to prevent?
Wearing sunglasses on the bus on my way to school.	If I take off the sunglasses, I might have to make eye contact with people, and then I'll have to talk to them.
Taking out my phone in line or in the elevator.	If I'm not looking at my phone, people might force me to make small talk.
Pretending I'm sick to avoid social events.	If I'm at home, I'm safe from the social situations that make me anxious.

What Are Your Safety Behaviors Costing You?

Avoidance and safety behaviors might be costing you more than you think. It's like being caught in a loop of self-sabotage. Your brain convinces you that socializing is dangerous, so you cling to your safety behaviors like a life raft in choppy waters.

But the more you cling to them, the more your brain believes the danger is real. When you allow yourself to keep falling back into your safety behaviors, you're reinforcing what your brain already believes—the situation is dangerous, and you need help! But if the goal is to get over the anxiety caused by socializing, then you've got to interrupt that thought pattern.

In essence, when you let yourself fall into the safety behaviors repeatedly, you're making the problem worse. You're allowing yourself to get stuck in your anxious thoughts, therefore missing out on the opportunity to engage with the people and conversations around you.

And since you don't have to engage with others, you mistakenly believe the safety behaviors work! But in reality, you're just reinforcing the behaviors so that they keep happening over and over again, so that you never really manage the anxiety that drives them. It's a vicious cycle that can be hard to break.

Take a moment to think about these questions:

- How does avoiding social interactions affect your friendships?

- Do safety behaviors have an impact on your confidence level? How so?

- Do safety behaviors solve the problem? Is it possible they're actually making the problem worse?

How Social Anxiety Works

Social anxiety can be a tricky beast to tame. It's not just the fear of social interaction that gets us, but the anticipation of it. We start analyzing every potential threat, from the possibility of awkwardness to full-blown humiliation, and before we know it, our brains are in full-blown panic mode.

Let's be honest, no one wants to feel embarrassed or awkward, so it makes sense that you want to avoid feeling that way.

And that's when you go into escape mode. You might manage to avoid meaningful conversations, having to look someone in the face, or giving that class presentation—but at what cost? Your confidence eventually decreases, your physical symptoms worsen when you can't escape social situations, and you increasingly rely on your safety behaviors. And then the cycle begins again.

The Vicious Cycle

The cycle of anxiety is reinforced by four components:

- Thoughts
- Feelings
- Physical Sensations
- Behaviors

Think back to Jeremy's story and you'll see it in action.

Jeremy decided to fake a stomachache after arriving at Ashton's party because he was getting increasingly anxious about having to talk to the guests at the party (especially once the girls came over).

As a result, he decided to leave early.

Once he got home, he felt a sense of relief that he had gotten out of the situation. But that feeling came at a cost—he proved to his brain that the situation was a threat, and as such, it noted the danger of small gatherings for next time.

Next time he has to face the same situation, his brain will flag this as a danger and he'll say to himself: "Remember when we had to fake stomachache to avoid it? Probably not a good idea to be in that situation again." So it's only natural that he will keep dodging it again, and keeping the cycle of anxiety going until the thought of socializing becomes unbearable.

The more effort you put into escaping the situation, the more dangerous your brain perceives it to be.

That's how the cycle works—first, you have an anxious thought about the situation, then negative feelings overwhelm you. Next, your body starts to react to the emotions, and then you resort to your safety behaviors.

And since the safety behaviors continue to drive your anxious thoughts and feelings, you're unknowingly keeping the cycle alive!

THE CYCLE OF ANXIETY EXPLAINED

- I will embarrass myself
- People will judge me
- Something will go wrong
- They will think I'm boring

Our behavior confirms our thoughts, and so our thoughts become stronger and the cycle intensifies

Our thoughts affect how we feel

THOUGHTS

- Avoid or escape situation
- Rely on safety behaviors
- Isolating from people
- Ask for reassurance

BEHAVIORS

FEELINGS

- Fear
- Extreme worry
- Anxiety
- Dread
- Panic

Our mental and physical feelings affect how we behave

PHYSICAL SYMPTOMS

When we feel we're in danger, our body goes on fight, flight or freeze mode

- Racing heart
- Sweating
- Shaking
- Shallow breaths
- Dizziness
- Stomach butterflies
- Blackout

The End of Chapter 1

If you're struggling with social anxiety, it can be tempting just to try to "tough it out" and hope that things will eventually get better on their own. But the truth is, ignoring social anxiety and hoping it will go away is like ignoring a broken bone and hoping it will heal on its own.

Getting help for social anxiety is important because:

- SAD can have a profound impact on your quality of life. If you're avoiding social situations, you can't fully participate in the activities and relationships that are important to you.
- SAD can lead to secondary problems, such as depression, substance abuse, and social isolation.

The good news is that social anxiety is highly treatable. With effort, you can learn how to manage your symptoms and eventually lead a healthy life. If you're ready to get started on the road to recovery, the first step is to seek guidance on what it is, how it works, and how to manage it.

But, hey, you've already taken that step since you're reading this right now.

CHAPTER 2

Rewire Your Brain

Isa's Invitation

The next day, Isa dragged herself out of bed, feeling like a wilted flower. She knew the day ahead was full of more social interactions, and the mere thought of it made her stomach turn.

Once again, she headed straight for her mom's makeup drawer, armed with creams and powders like a warrior preparing for battle. With a few well-placed swipes of makeup, she thought, she could at least try to hide her awkwardness and blend in with the crowd.

"Isa, don't forget that I packed a lunch for you today," her mother called as she headed for the door. "I saw that the one I packed for you yesterday was still in your backpack. Did you eat the school lunch, then?"

Isa gulped.

"Uh, yeah, it was fine. I won't forget the lunch you made for me today," Isa lied, feeling ashamed. She didn't feel good about fibbing to her mother, but it was easier than explaining her aversion to eating in the cafeteria with the other kids.

The mere thought of walking into the cafeteria sent her anxiety skyrocketing. Her brain played out endless scenarios of embarrassment and shame, each one more terrifying than the last.

In truth, she'd skipped lunch the day before. Instead, she had retreated to the sanctuary of the library, where the smell of books replaced the odor of stale cafeteria food, and the silence was a balm for her frayed nerves. Sure, she had to endure the piercing glare of the ancient librarian, old Mrs. Cranklebee, every time she so much as made a peep. But it was still better than the alternative of embarrassing herself at lunch.

After her mother dropped her off at school, Isa dug her headphones out of her backpack and popped them over her ears right away. The headphones were like a shield, protecting her from the outside world and the fear of being rejected. She knew that if she took them off, the noise of the hallway would be overwhelming, and that would affect her thinking. The other kids seemed like a different species, with their effortless socializing and easy smiles.

Why couldn't she find friendships that felt so seamlessly enjoyable?

Because, a voice piped up in her head, *you're too awkward to be likable.*

She turned up the music on her headphones.

As she unpacked her things at her locker, she stopped for a moment to stare at the paper lunch bag her mother had prepared for her. The lunch bag looked like a time bomb, ticking away the seconds until Isa would have to face her fears again. Even thinking about her lunch period made her stomach twist into knots. There was just no way she could bring herself to eat in the cafeteria, and food wasn't allowed in the library.

Isa sighed and tossed the lunch bag into the trash so her mother wouldn't find it again. As she turned around from the garbage can, she saw a hand waving in her face.

"Isa, is that you?"

Caught by surprise, Isa slipped off her headphones to find a girl with short chestnut brown hair and rosy cheeks smiling brightly at her.

"Chloe—uh—hi," Isa stammered. Isa's face turned a shade of red so deep it could have passed for a ripe tomato, and she desperately prayed that the layers of makeup she had applied earlier would conceal her embarrassment.

"You look so—different, like you got a makeover," Chloe said, eyebrows raised.

Chloe and Isa had played on the middle school basketball team together, but they hadn't seen each other for months after summer break started.

"Anyway," Chloe continued, "I'm having some of the girls from the team over to shoot hoops after school. You remember where I live? You should stop by, let's see if you're still any good," Chloe teased.

Isa stood there, frozen like a deer caught in headlights, her mind frantically searching for an excuse to avoid accepting the invite. She imagined how each one might sound …

Sorry, I got these weird purple and green welts all over and my mom has to take me to the doctor.

Oh man, wish I could, but I have to take my new pet lizard for a walk.

I totally would—but my brother just sprouted a tail overnight and researchers are coming to the house to find out why. You know how it is!

But nothing Isa came up with in the moment felt convincing enough. So instead she whispered, "Um, yeah, sure, see ya there," and dashed off to her first class.

Jeremy's First Day of School

Jeremy's eyes flickered open as he heard the blaring sound of his alarm clock. He groaned and slammed his hand down on the snooze button, trying to ignore the creeping sense of dread that had settled in the pit of his stomach.

Today was the first day of 10th grade, and he couldn't shake the feeling that everyone would be talking about his humiliating performance at Ashton's party. He couldn't believe he had made such a fool of himself in front of his classmates.

He mentally combed through every physical ailment he could possibly think of to get out of going to school, but his parents had long caught onto this trick. He knew it wouldn't work. The only option was to face the music and hope for the best.

Jeremy slipped into a dark sweatshirt and pulled the hood tightly around his face. The sweatshirt swallowed him up like a black hole. He felt like a ninja, ready to sneak past his classmates without being noticed.

The ride to school was solemn, as though he was headed towards his own funeral. He imagined what all the other kids must be feeling at this moment—excitement about seeing their friends, elation about meeting new friends, mild annoyance that summer had come to an end.

In Jeremy's mind, he was the only one drowning in a sea of dread and torment at the thought of returning to school.

Once he arrived at school, Jeremy's heart began to race. The first few steps through the hallways felt as though he was wading through quicksand. His hood was still pulled up, his face hidden from view. He didn't want to be noticed, didn't want to be seen as the awkward, embarrassing kid from the party. His eyes darted from side to side looking for any sign of Ashton and his friends—looking for any sign of danger.

"Hey, Jeremy!"

The color drained from Jeremy's face as he recognized Ashton's voice.

He'd been spotted.

Before he could put much thought into what to do, Jeremy sprang into action. He pretended he hadn't heard his name being shouted across the hallway. He darted into the first bathroom he could find and barricaded himself into a bathroom stall. His heart pounded in his chest and he could feel his hands shaking as though he'd just outrun the boogeyman. As he tried to catch his breath, he heard the warning bell for first period.

It was too risky to leave the bathroom now—what if Ashton was passing by the bathroom just as he came out and they had to come face-to-face?

Great! Late on the first day of school.

Jeremy sank to the floor, wishing he could make himself disappear.

The Cycle of Anxiety (Isn't Fun)

Remember the cycle of anxiety we talked about in Chapter 1?

Don't worry—this isn't a quiz. Here's a refresher!

Your thoughts are a powerful source of the anxiety you feel in any given situation. They feed into your feelings, which feed into your behaviors, and then the cycle starts over again.

How the cycle of anxiety works:

- Your thoughts influence your feelings and emotions.
- Your feelings and emotions influence how you behave.
- Your behaviors then influence the way you think about social situations, and the cycle begins again.

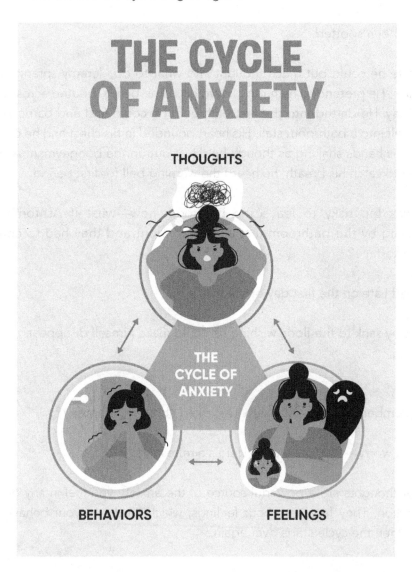

Consider Isa and Jeremy.

As soon as Isa arrives at school, she starts having anxious thoughts.

- She tells herself that she's too awkward to be likable.
- This thought causes her to feel a sense of dread when she thinks of talking to people in the hallways and in the cafeteria.
- These emotions drive her to put in her headphones as soon as she gets to school in the morning.

Then she engages in more behaviors to avoid socializing (for example, throwing her lunch away to avoid the cafeteria, and continuing to put her headphones over her ears) and the cycle gets worse with each passing day.

The reality is that anyone would be lucky to have Isa as a friend. She's a kind, fun, and interesting person (just like you!) However, because she believes her thoughts and they feel real to her, she doesn't believe she's cool enough to have friends like everyone else.

So what about Jeremy—is he caught in the cycle of anxiety, too?

After the party, Jeremy fell into a trap that might sound familiar. He spent hours pouring over every moment he could remember at Ashton's party and because he thought he humiliated himself, he assumed it must be true.

As a result, he feels embarrassed and anxious about seeing Ashton and his friends at school. So when Ashton greets him the next day, he makes a run for it, further isolating himself from a friend group that might otherwise welcome him with open arms.

Both Jeremy and Isa are trapped in the cycle of anxiety because they engage in avoidance behaviors. **Avoidance** is a coping mechanism that brings you short-term relief from anxiety—but ends up hurting you in the long run.

The cycle of social anxiety, and the avoidance behaviors that come with it, cost you long-term growth by denying you opportunities for exposure to other people. Your brain wants the immediate relief of escape, and each time you grant it that relief, the experience of anxiety intensifies the next time you feel the discomfort.

When you learn to confront your fears and cope with the short-term increase in anxiety, your confidence stabilizes, and the hamster wheel of the anxiety cycle is broken. In other words, you can separate the connection between your thoughts, feelings, and behaviors by changing your thoughts.

That's where Cognitive Behavioral Therapy (CBT) comes in.

Your Brain and Cognitive Behavioral Therapy

Have you ever thought that you can predict the future?

Fortune-telling is an unhelpful thinking pattern describing people who think they can predict what will happen in the future, such as an upcoming social situation or event. Fortune-telling mainly fixates on anticipating negativity.

For example, Jeremy believes that he knows what will happen if he talks to Ashton and his friend group at school—he just knows that he'll humiliate himself and that the guys will dislike him.

But he's wrong.

Listen, you're good at so many things. But predicting the future *isn't* one of them.

If you're anything like Jeremy and you're starting to think your brain is messed up—think again! Although it's not technically a muscle, your brain can be exercised as if you're training to run a marathon. Think of Cognitive Behavioral Therapy (CBT) as the "weights" used for someone who is building body muscle...in their brain.

CBT is a simple intervention that takes our brains out of the social anxiety cycle and into a healthy space. It helps you identify negative thoughts and beliefs, challenge them, and decrease them over time.

The theory is that if you can change your thinking, you can change your life. That means you will feel better if you maintain healthy thinking habits and coping behaviors. Doing so reduces the frequency and intensity with which you experience anxiety—almost like magic!

Your Mind Has Superpowers

Okay, so it doesn't *actually* have magical superpowers (that we know of). But your brain *is* super powerful.

Your brain is the control center of your entire body. It tells you what to think, how to feel, and what to do (whether you're actively aware of it or not).

Let's put your brain's "superpowers" to the test.

Close your eyes and imagine a plate of the most incredible tacos you've ever had. Each crunchy shell is stuffed to the max with warm, ooey-gooey-cheesy goodness and fresh, tangy salsa. You grab a large bottle of your favorite sauce and drizzle it on top before taking a big savory bite.

Is your mouth salivating as you imagine the tacos? Crazy, right?

41

You aren't actually sitting in front of a delicious plate of tacos. And yet, the first step in the digestion process has already begun. Your brain has tricked itself into believing that you're about to eat something that doesn't even exist!

Unfortunately, this doesn't just apply to thoughts about delicious food—it also applies to thoughts about ourselves and situations that may or may not exist.

If you close your eyes and imagine yourself immersed in one of your worst fears, your body will respond to that, too. Do you hate snakes or spiders? Do you have a fear of heights or small, cramped spaces?

If you're up for it, take a moment to visualize yourself trapped in a pit of slithering snakes and hairy, scuttling spiders. Imagine standing at the edge of a skyscraper looking down or lying in a tiny, cramped hole with no way to get out.

Okay, now snap out of it—if you linger in these thoughts for too long, you'll eventually start feeling symptoms of distress. Your heart rate might climb, you may start sweating, and you'll experience other symptoms of physical discomfort.

That's because your brain is like a supercomputer, and the way you talk to yourself is how you "program" your brain to operate. So whether you feed your brain images of delicious tacos or negative self-talk about the danger of social situations, it's going to listen.

But here's the thing—as powerful as it can be, a thought is just a thought. It's not always accurate or helpful (that is making you salivate for an imaginary plate of tacos or panic about imaginary snakes and spiders). But you can learn to control how your thoughts work, and "reprogram" how your brain responds to better cope with SAD, by challenging negative thoughts when they occur.

Stop Letting Your Mind Play Tricks

Quick—don't think of a bright orange monkey eating a banana!

You couldn't *not* think about a bright orange monkey eating a banana once you read it in the sentence, right?

Imagine Isa avoiding lunch to read a book and telling herself *don't think about embarrassing yourself in front of your classmates.*

Or, Jeremy on the way to Ashton's birthday repeating the thought, *don't think about saying something awkward at a party.*

Both of them tried it, and both of them wound up obsessively thinking about exactly the thing they didn't want to do, until it began to feed their cycle of anxiety.

Once you start thinking about something, it feels impossible not to think about it. And even if you make a plan to make the thoughts go away, you'll wind up feeling more anxiety about them because it's not possible to *not* think about something once the thought is already there.

Don't let yourself get caught in this vicious cycle.

Instead, let's talk about how you can stop negative thoughts in their tracks and begin reprogramming your thinking.

Steps For Defeating Negative Thought Patterns

Think of defeating negative thought patterns as a weight-lifting exercise for your brain:

1. Identify and acknowledge your negative thoughts.
2. Engage in cognitive defusion: Realize your thoughts aren't you.
3. Challenge your thoughts.

You may not realize it, but many of your thoughts are on autopilot. Some research suggests that up to 90% of our thoughts are repetitive, so if you're prone to negative thinking, your brain will create unique neural pathways to make it easier for you to produce those negative thoughts.

Following those three simple steps will make it easier to break the "stinking thinking" that causes you problems.

So let's take a closer look at each step:

Step 1: Identify and Acknowledge: Do Not Avoid!

Once you can master *not* trying to avoid your negative thoughts, you'll be surprised at how much relief you feel. When you try to avoid your negative thoughts, you stress yourself out more and miss the opportunity to practice acceptance.

Negative thoughts are a survival mechanism built into your brain to alert you when something isn't quite right.

> Rather than trying to avoid your anxious negative thoughts, acknowledge that you're just having *"thoughts"* and thank them for popping into your mind. After all, they're trying to protect you!

But remember, negative thoughts don't have to run the show.

For example, imagine if Isa had simply acknowledged her anxiety about interacting with her classmates at school instead of pushing the thought from her mind and hiding out in the library. Or what if Jeremy had identified his anxious thoughts about humiliating himself in front of Ashton at school as just that—thoughts—rather than cold, hard facts?

Isa could have eaten lunch in the cafeteria and made friends with the kids in her grade, and Jeremy could have had a conversation with Ashton, only to realize Ashton actually thinks he's pretty cool.

They would have discovered their brains were simply playing tricks on them. And by reading rest of this chapter, you can overcome the tricks your brain plays, too.

Step 2: Cognitive Defusion: Your Thoughts Are Not You!

After accepting the negative thoughts and acknowledging their presence, the second step is to separate yourself from your thoughts. This is called "Cognitive Defusion," or "Thought Distancing".

It's like imagining yourself as a fly on the wall of your own life, rather than seeing yourself as the main character.

In this step, you recognize your negative thoughts and feelings as internal constructs (in other words, things you imagine rather than things that are real), but not as foundations that drive your behavior. Cognitive defusion gives you the opportunity to choose how to respond to a situation rather than allowing yourself to behave defensively and unintentionally.

> You can create space between yourself and your thoughts by using phrases such as "I am feeling…" **or** "I am having the thought that…"
> **Instead of saying** "I'm…" or "I will…"

For example, instead of saying "I'm anxious and scared, I will freeze in today's presentation," you can say "I'm feeling anxious, I'm having the thought that I might freeze in today's presentation."

This way you're creating distance between yourself and your thoughts. And the more you do this, the more your brain realizes that your thoughts are not you.

You start to gain perspective so that you can judge situations better, and build emotional resilience, so that your emotions don't run away with you.

> You can even name your negative thoughts to help you remember that they aren't a reflection of who you are as a person!

Since Isa is a basketball player, she might name her thoughts Flop. A "flop" in basketball is when one player tricks the referee and audience into believing that another player has committed a foul—but in reality, none has been committed at all!

So, Flop is a fitting name for Isa's negative thinking.

The next time Isa recognizes a negative thought about embarrassing herself at school, she might say, "Oh, there's Flop again. What do you have to offer me today, buddy?"

In doing so, Isa could see that her thoughts are separate from her—and that they're only temporary.

Reading about cognitive defusion may be easy. But just like preparing to run a marathon, it takes some work to apply in real life.

So let's try a short practice activity to start building some mental muscle.

Exercise: Cognitive Defusion Practice

Here's a quick exercise you can do the next time you spot negative thoughts, to start building the strength to combat them. For this practice, think of a negative thought you had earlier today.

1. **Have a seat in a comfortable position.**
   Close your eyes and start bringing awareness to your breathing.

2. **Begin acknowledging your thought.**
   For example, "I'm having the thought that…" or "I notice I'm feeling…" instead of "I am…" or "I will…"

3. **Accept and acknowledge your thoughts.**
   Remind yourself they're not true just because they exist. Thank your thought for making itself known.

4. **Visualize the space your negative thought takes up in your mind.**
   Now, imagine it's shrinking down, down, down… until it becomes as small as a tiny (but annoying) mosquito. Give the mosquito a name and challenge it with a statement to put it in its place. For example, "You're just a thought, you Measly Mosquito—you don't define my reality."

5. **Refocus your thoughts on your breathing.**
   As the thoughts begin to lose their power, ask yourself if they are serving you. Are they accurate? Are you trying to predict the future? Are you imagining the worst-case scenario?

If Jeremy performed this exercise, here's how it might look for him:

1. *I'm breathing in and counting to three. Then, I'm breathing out and counting to five. My breaths are calm and controlled.*
2. *I notice I'm feeling anxious about seeing Ashton at school after the birthday party. I'm having the thought that I always humiliate myself in social situations.*
3. *Thanks, thoughts, for making yourself known—I know that you're only trying to protect me. I acknowledge your presence in my brain, but I know you aren't necessarily true, simply because you exist.*
4. *This thought takes up a lot of space in my mind, but now it's shrinking down to a speck. It's buzzing around like an annoying mosquito—I'm going to call it Manny the Mosquito. Manny, you're just taking up space in my brain, and I know you mean well, but you aren't accurately reflecting my reality.*
5. *I'm still breathing in and counting to three, and counting to five as I exhale. These thoughts about humiliating myself in front of Ashton and his friends don't actually serve me. I'm trying to predict a future which hasn't even happened yet, and I'm no fortune teller.*

Step 3: Challenge Your Thoughts: Is Your Mind Tricking You Again?

Acknowledging thoughts and separating ourselves from that voice in our head are important steps, but that's not enough. It's time to challenge the thoughts.

Learning how to challenge our distorted thoughts is the step that will help us to reduce the effects negative thoughts have on us. Here are some steps you can take when facing unpleasant thoughts:

A. Identify and Label Cognitive Distortions

We call automatic negative thoughts **cognitive distortions**, and they are the root of many mental health issues, such as anxiety, depression, and emotional distress. If you're aware of the cognitive distortions that contribute to SAD, you can start to challenge and reframe those thoughts.

Doing so can help reduce your distress and improve your overall well-being—so why wouldn't you want to do it?

So, the next time your brain starts telling you all the reasons why you're not good enough, remember that cognitive distortion is just a trick of the mind, and *don't fall for it.*

Instead, take a step back and sit with those thoughts without judgment. Identify each thought as negative and acknowledge its presence in your mind—but know that you don't have to believe it to be true.

One way to make challenging your thoughts easier is knowing how to label them.

Here is a list of labels for some common cognitive distortions that people often experience, along with definitions and examples of thoughts:

Fortune-Telling

Jumping to conclusions about things that haven't happened; making assumptions about what others are thinking.

- *My teacher is going to tell me I failed the test.*

- *The other kids at school are going to think I'm awkward.*

Catastrophizing

Combination of fortune-telling and all-or-nothing thinking; blowing things out of proportion; assuming the worst possible outcome.

- *This spot on my skin is probably skin cancer; I'll be dead soon.*
- *I just blew my one shot at having friends in high school.*

Black and White Thinking

All or nothing thinking that doesn't consider any kind of in-between scenario.

- *I never have anything interesting to say.*
- *I always humiliate myself whenever I open my mouth.*

Labeling

Labeling yourself in a negative way; affects how you feel about yourself in different contexts.

- *I'm just not a healthy person.*
- *I'm not the kind of person that others want to be friends with.*

Mental Filter

Only seeing and obsessing about the negative aspect of a situation and not noticing the positives.

- *I can never do anything right.*

- *Everything went wrong.*

Overgeneralization

Applying your experience from one situation or event to all other situations or events.

- *I failed a test—I'll never get into college.*

- *She didn't ask me to hang out, nobody wants to be friends with me.*

Personalization

Blaming yourself for things that are outside of your direct control.

- *Our team lost because of me.*

- *He didn't sit next to me in class, I must have done something wrong.*

Magnification and minimization

Exaggerating the negative aspect of a situation and downplaying the positive.

- *We only had one good conversation—it's not like we're going to be friends.*

- *I answered a question correctly in class, but it doesn't mean I'm smart.*

Comparison

Comparing just one part of your performance or situation to another's so that it makes you appear in a negative light.

- *All of my friends are happier than me.*

- *Everyone else makes friends so easily.*

Challenge: Spot the Distortion

Now that you've learned about some of the cognitive distortions, can you spot the ones we've seen in Isa and Jeremy's stories so far?

- Isa knows that if she eats lunch in the cafeteria, she'll humiliate herself and never make any friends.

- As Jeremy walks into school, he looks around and assumes that everyone except for him has an easy time making new friends.

- Isa believes that every time she opens her mouth to talk, she embarrasses herself.

- Jeremy tells himself he's a socially awkward freak.

How did you do?

1. Catastrophizing and Fortune-Telling
2. Comparison
3. Black and White Thinking
4. Labeling

B. Gain Perspective and Check Your Reality

Negative thinking is like a pesky little goblin that sneaks into your brain and starts wreaking havoc. But don't worry, you can kick that little trouble-maker to the curb by **conducting a "brain Interview".** *In other words, you can ask a series of tough questions to challenge your thoughts. Are these thoughts legit or just anxious fictions?*

Don't let that goblin control your thoughts—be the boss of your own brain!

It's best to focus on one negative thought at a time, so complete this exercise as often as needed to address each of the individual negative thoughts that pop into your head throughout the day.

Challenge: Brain Interview

First, write down a negative thought you had today.

For example, *I never know what to say when other people talk to me*, or, *I'm the worst math student in the whole school.*

Negative Thought:

_____

_____

Now, answer these questions one by one, to challenge the negative thought and see it from a different perspective.

What factual information backs up this thought?

_____

_____

What evidence contradicts this thought?

_____

_____

Am I overgeneralizing based on unrelated events that have happened in the past?

_____

_____

If I have to take another look at this from a positive perspective, what would I see?

_____

_____

Am I going to care about this a week, a month, or a year from now?

_____

_____

What advice would I give a friend going through this experience?

_____

_____

Are my thoughts being helpful or are they making the situation worse? How?

_____

_____

Am I using phrases like "never," "always," "must," or "have to" in my thinking right now?

_____

_____

Besides me, what else is affecting the situation?

_____

_____

What does the worst-case scenario look like?

_____

_____

What does the best-case scenario look like?

_____

_____

If I try to be objective, what is likely to happen?

_____

_____

Now that you've identified the thought as negative and gone through the questions, you may have realized that this is just a temporary thought, and you may have come up with a perspective that wasn't there initially.

You might have managed to see the situation for what it really is, rather than allowing your thoughts about hopes and fears to rule your behaviors.

Another fun way to explore whether your thought is based in reality, or if it's driven by anxiety, is a process called **"reality checking."**

Reality checking helps you decide whether your negative thoughts are dominating, controlling, or overwhelming your logical thinking and forcing you to imagine the worst case scenario. It helps you tell the difference between which thoughts are real and which ones aren't, so you can judge the situation realistically and eventually alter how you behave in challenging situations.

Challenge: Jeremy's Reality Checking Courtroom

This challenge goes like this:

First, you're going to look at Jeremy's current situation at school (in case you forgot, he's currently hiding out in the bathroom, late to class on the first day, all to avoid running into Ashton).

Then, you're going to pretend you're a judge and his negative thoughts about what is happening around him are pleading their case. You'll look at the facts and judge whether his thoughts are based in reality or not!

Here are some steps to help you "reality check"
Jeremy's thinking:

Steps For Reality Checking:

1. Consider the situation from as many points of view as possible.
2. Fact-check the thoughts.
3. Consider the current reaction—is Jeremy reacting too much, just right, or not enough? Imagine all possible reactions.

Ready? Here we go!

NEGATIVE THOUGHT:

Your honor, Jeremy is a weirdo. He went to Ashton's birthday party and couldn't even make it through the party without embarrassing himself and having to leave early. No one at the party likes him anymore, and if he runs into Ashton and his friends at school, then Jeremy will only embarrass himself some more, so he belongs in that bathroom stall, hiding from the world.

Using the steps outlined above, take a moment to craft a response to this negative thought using Reality Checking.

YOU BE THE JUDGE:

_____

_____

_____

_____

_____

Example response on the next page...

Did your response sound something like this?

"Your claim that Jeremy left the party early is true, but the rest of your claim may not be. Let's look at things from Ashton's perspective. Ashton approached Jeremy at school to say hello, so it seems he still wants to be friends with Jeremy.

I find that your claim that no one likes Jeremy anymore isn't based in fact. Jeremy's reaction, in hiding in the bathroom and being late to class, is pretty extreme for the situation, and it seems he's reacting to his social anxiety rather than a situation that's based in reality. Running into Ashton won't actually make things worse. He's fortune telling.

I rule that this thinking is NOT based in reality! Negative thought dismissed."

Okay, your turn.

Challenge: Your Reality Checking Courtroom

Imagine a negative thought you had today. Using the same steps as those above, be your own judge and Reality Check whether it's based in reality or simply a result of anxious thinking.

_____

_____

_____

_____

_____

C. Replace Blue Thoughts with True Thoughts

Once you realize the thoughts in your head aren't real, it's time to replace them with more helpful ways of thinking. Replacing your overly negative thinking with realistic alternatives will inspire you to take positive actions and start creating the kind of life you actually want to live.

Replacing your negative thoughts literally retrains your brain to see the bright side of things, and to stop assuming there's danger lurking around every dark corner (or in any social situation!)

Challenge: Blue to True

In this activity, you'll write your negative thoughts on the left side of the column. Then, you'll challenge the thought with a more realistic and hopeful replacement thought on the right side.

First, here are some examples!

Negative Thought	Reflections About This Thought	Positive Replacement Thought
EXAMPLE: If I ask a girl out on a date, she'll say no, and I'll be doomed to die alone.	This thought is fortune-telling mixed with catastrophizing. I don't have any evidence that it's true.	I will ask out the girl I like. There's a chance she will say yes! But if she says no, it's not the end of the world—I will ask someone else next time. It's not going to kill me to get rejected.
EXAMPLE: I'm such an awkward person, I don't deserve to have any friends.	This thought is labeling and overgeneralization. This is just a negative thought I have about myself, but it doesn't necessarily mean others are thinking the same about me.	The truth is everybody does awkward things sometimes. If I do say something awkward, people will likely laugh it off and forget about it. I would be a good friend to have.

Your turn!

There's no time limit, so take your time and feel free to come back to this page and work on it more than once!

Negative Thought	Reflections About This Thought	Positive Replacement Thought

The End of Chapter 2

We've all been there before—the heart racing, the palms sweating, the mind going blank. For some of us, social anxiety happens regularly. Social anxiety is the fear of social situations, specifically those in which others may judge us. This fear is caused by cognitive distortions or negative and distorted thinking.

If our distorted thoughts go unchecked, we create a self-fulfilling cycle of anxiety. In other words, our negative thinking creates an anxious response, reinforcing our negative thinking. This cycle can be challenging to break out of, but with awareness and effort, it's possible to silence that pesky inner voice—finally.

Pro-Tip: Practice, practice, practice.

The only way to better manage your cognitive distortions is to practice identifying and challenging them. So commit yourself to identifying and challenging at least one cognitive distortion daily. And before you know it, you'll be a pro at managing your negative thoughts!

Here's a summary of how to deal with negative thoughts:

Step 1—Identify and acknowledge your thoughts.

- ○ *Do not try to avoid your thoughts.*
- ○ *Label them as "thoughts."*
- ○ *Thank them for stopping by.*

Step 2—Engage in cognitive defusion.

- ○ *Use phrases such as "I feel" rather than "I am."*
- ○ *Name your negative thoughts.*
- ○ *Visualize your negative thought as a different entity with distinct features.*

Step 3—Challenge your thoughts.

- ○ *Identify your cognitive distortions: Do you notice yourself fortune telling? Or catastrophizing?*
- ○ *Interview your brain by asking yourself a series of questions to gain perspective and train your mind to be objective, and think about your answers.*
- ○ *Attend the Reality Checking courtroom and think about how a judge would respond. Is this thought based in reality, or are there facts to back it up?*
- ○ *Replace blue thoughts with true thoughts and come up with alternative possibilities. There might be more logical outcomes that you're ruling out.*

CHAPTER 3

Calm Your Body

Isa and Chloe

As Isa huddled in the stacks of the library, she strategized like a military commander trying to avoid enemy fire.

How could she slip past Chloe and her basketball squad without getting caught in a barrage of small talk and awkward chit-chat with strangers? Isa had to admit, she missed being part of the group, but the idea of facing an unknown number of unfamiliar faces was enough to make her consider enrolling in witness protection.

Isa suspected there would be people she didn't know hanging out at Chloe's house after school, and she *hated* the thought of talking to a bunch of strangers.

Isa just knew she would end up embarrassing herself because it had happened before. She shivered as she remembered last summer's 8th grade slumber party.

On the last day of school, Chloe had invited Isa to a celebration sleepover. Chloe promised it would just be Isa and a few girls from their basketball team, so Isa accepted.

But she soon discovered Chloe hadn't been entirely truthful. There were a couple of girls Isa knew and liked from the basketball team. But unfortunately, Chloe had also invited her friends from dance class.

"I thought you wouldn't come if I told you about the dance girls," Chloe said apologetically. "But it will be fun, they're all really nice."

That turned out to be less than truthful as well. When Chloe introduced Isa to her other friends, a lanky girl with shiny black hair whispered something that made the other girls laugh.

Isa had a nasty feeling that whatever the joke was, it had been at her own expense.

Feeling humiliated, Isa spent the rest of the evening reading a book with her headphones on while the other girls played board games and watched movies. After the slumber party, Isa made a plan to avoid Chloe for the rest of the summer.

And avoiding Chloe had worked so far—until today. By the time the dismissal bell rang, Isa headed to her locker feeling torn about what to do and *very* hungry from skipping lunch.

"Hey, Isa!"

Chloe hurried over and leaned against the lockers, smiling excitedly and motioning for Isa to take off her headphones.

"I'm so excited you're coming over. Want to grab ice cream at that shop around the corner on the way home? I went with my family a few times over the summer—best chocolate-chip-cookie-dough ice cream in the world."

Isa's stomach grumbled. At the words "chocolate-chip-cookie-dough," she knew she was at least willing to swing by the ice cream shop with her old friend. But there was still one thing she needed to know.

She had to find out who Chloe had invited over. The thought of running into the girls from dance class (or anyone else she didn't know, for that matter) was simply unbearable.

"How are you liking high school so far?" Chloe asked as they headed up the street. "I love it," she went on before Isa could answer, "There's so many new people to talk to."

"Uh, it's fine. I like my math class," Isa mumbled.

"Of course you do, you've always been good at math. Who do you sit with at lunch? I tried to find you today," Chloe said, raising an eyebrow.

"Oh, I just kind of hung out in the library and listen to music during lunch."

Isa thought to herself: *Now she's really going to think I'm weird.*

"What? No way. I heard that old librarian is a real bummer. You have to come sit with me tomorrow!"

Isa forced herself to smile—Mrs. Cranklebee was definitely a bummer to spend time with every day. But there were probably a hundred people at Chloe's lunch table, and it made Isa's stomach feel queasy just thinking about it.

"So who all is coming over later?" Isa asked, hoping to divert Chloe's attention away from the topic of lunch.

"Just a few girls from the team, like I said. Oh, here's the place—best ice cream in town!"

They headed into the shop. Freezers whirred noisily as Isa took in the colorful array of flavors before her, and Chloe ran right up to the counter to order two scoops of chocolate chip cookie dough.

"And for you?"

In a flash, it was Isa's turn to order, and she had absolutely no clue what to say.

She looked up at the menu board, but it seemed to blur together in a jumble of letters and prices. A few awkward seconds went by and the man behind the counter cleared his throat. Isa felt his eyes on her, waiting for her to speak. She could practically *hear* the seconds ticking by, and each one seemed to be counting down to her inevitable embarrassment.

Why can't I just be one of those people who orders right away? What's wrong with me?

"She's never been here before, first time," Chloe interjected.

"I see, want to try some samples? They're free," the man offered.

Isa glanced around. They were the only ones in the shop—for now.

"There's unlimited samples. I tried every flavor last summer," Chloe added.

Isa shrugged and pointed to a few of the most tempting options. Rainbow Sorbet turned out to be too fruity, and Peanut Butter Dream was too salty.

Then at last, she came upon a mint chocolate chip flavor that tasted just like a real girl scout cookie.

"My second favorite flavor," Chloe chimed in as Isa let the sample melt on her tongue.

"Two scoops, please," Isa said, with a grin. She was finally starting to feel a bit more at ease.

Just then, the door chimed.

Isa turned to see a crowd of noisy classmates filing into the store. Chloe turned and her face lit up as she greeted all the people she recognized. Isa stood by watching and listening from the corner of the shop, ice cream in hand, dripping down the side of her fist as it melted.

Suddenly, ice cream didn't sound so good anymore.

"Yeah, I'm having some people over later. Wanna join? Isa's coming too," Chloe said.

"Who's Isa?"

"We played basketball together in middle school. She's incredible, never misses a shot." Motioning towards Isa.

Isa felt her face flush bright red as everyone turned to look at her.

Suddenly, a horrible vision entered her head. What if she went over to Chloe's house and had to prove she never missed a shot—and then missed every single shot?

She envisioned an endless crowd of Chloe's friends laughing at her as she chased a bouncing basketball around the driveway.

Nope, nope, nope. Abort mission.

"Um, actually, I—I think I'm going to head home," Isa muttered, heart pounding.

"Maybe next time, though. Thanks for the ice cream, Chloe. See you later." And with that, Isa hurried for the door before Chloe could try to change her mind.

Jeremy's First Class
The coast is probably clear now.

Jeremy slowly opened the door of the restroom and peaked around the corner. No sign of life. He felt relieved as he headed to class knowing there was no chance of running into Ashton or his friends.

But then it hit him.

I'm late to my first period class…on the first day of school.

The fear of opening the door and being the center of attention was more than he could bear. He imagined the worst possible outcomes, from being yelled at by the teacher to being laughed at by the entire class.

I'll probably have to change schools.

But when he finally opened the door to his first period science class, only a couple of students looked up from their work. No one laughed, and no one whispered about him. The teacher walked over to Jeremy and pointed him towards his desk. He didn't yell, and he didn't even seem angry.

"Get lost? Hi, I'm Mr. Garcia," the teacher said politely.

"We just got started on "About You" presentations. Directions are on the board, and you'll have one minute to present when it's your turn."

Jeremy's heart sank.

Presentations. One of the most dreaded activities in the history of education.

And of course, the universe had conspired to ensure that he had to do one on the very first day of school. It was like the educational demons were out to get him. He had somehow managed to avoid presentations his entire life, but now he had no good excuse to get out of this one.

"Mr. Garcia, I don't know if I'll have enough time to make a presentation since I'm late," Jeremy whispered, hoping he'd manage to wriggle his way out of it.

"You can achieve anything if you set your mind to it." Mr. Garcia said smartly.

"But sir," Jeremy continued desperately, "isn't this science class? Why do people need to learn about me?"

"This is biology class," Mr. Garcia corrected him. "We study living things, and you're alive, aren't you? And make sure you're on time tomorrow."

Dang, he's one sharp teacher.

Jeremy's mind was in a frenzy as he scrambled to put together a presentation about himself. He tried to focus on the task at hand, but he couldn't shake the image of himself standing at the front of the classroom, sweat pouring down his face, and his classmates snickering and whispering behind his back.

The ticking clock on the board only added to the pressure, and Jeremy felt like he was suffocating under the weight of his own anxiety. He couldn't help but feel like a bomb was about to explode.

"Time's up," Mr. Garcia said to the class after what felt like only a few seconds of work time.

Is anyone else freaking out about this as much as I am? What the heck is wrong with me?

"While you worked, I wrote your names on these slips," he said, motioning to a plastic bowl full of folded pieces of paper. "When I draw your name, you'll come up and present your "About Me" assignment to the class for one minute."

Jeremy felt his heart pound as he watched Mr. Garcia reach into the bowl of names.

Please don't pick me, please don't pick me, please don't pick ...

"Jeremy Carter, you're up."

Hearing his name hit him like a piano falling off a skyscraper—not only did Jeremy have to present in front of the class, but he had to go first.

How did I get so unlucky? What did I do to deserve this!

Jeremy's mouth went dry as he stood up and walked to the front of the room on knees made of jello. He felt like he was walking towards his own execution. A wave of nausea hit him as he noticed Ashton sitting in the front row looking back at him. Ashton gave him a small wave and a thumbs up, but Jeremy pretended he hadn't noticed.

"My name is Jeremy Carter," he began, reading off the page as though he might forget his own name.

A drop of sweat slid down his face as he glanced over the top of his paper and saw that everyone's eyes were on him. Jeremy gulped and quickly looked back down only to realize he lost his place.

"Uh, how old am I? Oh, right—I'm 16 years old."

Two girls giggled and turned to whisper to each other, and Jeremy noted with alarm that he recognized the strawberry blonde, Shania, from Ashton's party.

Wow, I thought this couldn't get any worse.

Jeremy's heart began beating so fast it felt as though it was about to jump out through his throat.

"I like—uh—I mean—well," he stopped. An icy feeling of dread crept through his body from bottom to top, taking hold in his chest. His mind blacked out completely and he froze, forgetting what to do or say next.

"What do you like to do for fun?" Mr. Garcia asked helpfully.

Jeremy couldn't find the words. He could feel the eyes of the other students watching his every move, and he wished he could just disappear.

"I'm sorry," he choked, not trusting himself to say anything more. And with that, he headed back to his desk and put his head down in shame.

"Alright then," Mr. Garcia said, confused. "Let's move on to our next presenter."

For the rest of the class, Jeremy kept his head down and tuned out the rest of the About Me presentations. If he hadn't, he'd have noticed a few of the other kids that messed up their presentations, too.

At last, the bell for second period rang. Jeremy slowly stood up and pulled up his hood once more, wishing the ground would open up and swallow him whole as he headed for the door.

"Jeremy," Mr. Garcia said before Jeremy could make his exit. "Come see me after school, I'd like you to give the whole presentation thing another shot. It's your first grade of the year, so it's worth it to do your best."

Jeremy couldn't believe it—he had to do it *again*? He nodded silently and thought to himself, *Now how am I supposed to get out of this one?*

Welcome to the Experiment

Have you ever done an experiment before? Humans are natural scientists, and we conduct experiments all the time—but we don't always realize we're doing it. Brains love experiments because they ultimately drive decisions about survival.

Consider what happened when Isa and Chloe went out for ice cream.

Chloe already knew her order—she found the best flavor in the shop last summer and she's sticking to it. Isa, who has never been to the shop before, had to test out a few flavors to see what she liked best. By taste-testing a few different ice creams, Isa's brain tested out which flavor reacted best with her taste buds.

In this chapter, you're going to let your brain do a kind of "taste test" with calming techniques. By the time you're done with this chapter, you'll know twelve new hacks to calm your body, and how to use them to feel more in control of SAD symptoms.

These soothing techniques are kind of like unlimited power ups in a video game—you can use them over and over, and they never run out. They give you the power you need to defeat the boss at the end of the level (your negative thoughts) so you can minimize your anxiety.

Remember, the cycle of anxiety is rooted in human traits that drive our survival instinct. If you're physically uncomfortable (heart racing, sweating, blushing, upset stomach, shaking, panicking) then your body goes into fight or flight mode, and your mind is too busy panicking and focusing on the body sensations to think logically.

But when your body is calm, your brain gives you more freedom to concentrate on the cognitive techniques you learned in Chapter 2—acknowledging anxious thoughts, defusing them, and challenging them.

So put on your white lab coat and grab your safety goggles—let's experiment with some different techniques and see what works best for you.

The Power of Breathing

Have you ever noticed what happens in your body when you're faced with stressful circumstances?

As soon as your brain detects danger, it sets off an alarm that kicks your nervous system into high gear. And since your nervous system is the queen bee of your body, you'd better believe every one of your other organs listens when it sends a message.

The stress hormone cortisol and the threat response hormone Adrenaline rush through your veins to get you ready to throw down in a fight, or fly like the wind, and before you know it, you start breathing harder and faster. And even though you probably know that interacting with people isn't dangerous, your body deals with it in the same way as if you were being charged by a pack of hungry wolves—by going into fight, flight, or freeze mode.

This process is the body's sympathetic response, and if you practice enough, you can learn to control it through breathing.

But we're not talking about any old breathing. We're talking about the five star, high-quality, crème-de-la-crème of breaths.

Deep, focused, fill-your-body-up breaths.

Calm, controlled breathing triggers a powerful response—one that convinces your brain that you're safe. It's your most powerful secret weapon when you notice you're feeling stressed or anxious.

Your brain on controlled breathing:
Once your brain gets the signal that everything is A-OK, your body goes through some incredible changes.

- First, your brain stops firing off high levels of stress hormones, and your body returns to normal functioning.
- Then, your blood pressure decreases, and your heart stops thumping in your chest.
- As you control your breath, levels of oxygen and carbon dioxide become more balanced, and give you a "clearer" head to think logically.
- Your blood resumes sending oxygen to all parts of your brain and body, giving you a boost in mood and energy.
- A feelings of calm takes over, and you experience a comforting sense of control over your situation.

And that's why controlled breathing is truly the greatest weapon you have in your arsenal when it comes to staying calm. Perhaps if Jeremy and Isa had known this technique, they would've been able to power through their situations more effectively without having to retreat.

There's more to it than mindlessly inhaling and exhaling, though. Like learning anything new, it takes regular practice. Once you get the hang of them, breathing exercises can be a powerful tool for managing your social anxiety symptoms.

Let's look at a few different breathing exercises that you can use any time you feel anxious, to help you overcome the physical symptoms of SAD and calm your body.

Breathing Exercises for Managing Negative Thoughts

Time to start the experiment we mentioned at the beginning of the chapter! You'll complete one of these anxiety measurement charts at the beginning and end of each section.

Rate how you feel before starting this section.

Smooth Sailing (No Anxiety)	Don't Love It (Some Anxiety)	Hate It (More Anxiety)	NOPE NOPE NOPE (High Anxiety)
0	1	2	3

Maybe you've tried breathing exercises before…and they didn't work.

It's frustrating when that happens. But if you're willing to give it a shot, these breathing exercises are, well, different. These exercises are easy, silly, and effective. As you try each one, imagine you're tucking it away into your mind like a power-up to use later.

Exercise: Lion's Breath

Have you ever seen a cat yawn? They really go for fangs out, tongue out, mouth opened wide, as far as they can go. This forceful exhalation helps you feel an immediate sense of release. That's the idea behind this silly yet effective breathing technique. If you're feeling anxious, try finding a quiet spot and following these steps.

Step 1: Kneel with your ankles crossed or sit criss-cross-apple-sauce.

Step 2: Place your hand on your knees. Take up as much space as you can by stretching out your arms and fingers.

Step 3: Inhale slowly and deeply.

Step 4: Fun part—exhale through your mouth and say "Ha!" Open your mouth as wide as you can and stick out your tongue towards your chin.

Step 5: Relax your face and do it a few times until you feel calmer.

Exercise: Alternate Nostril Breathing

This one is popular among some well-known pop singers and performance artists. It's a super effective yoga-based breathing exercise for slowing your heart rate and calming your nerves before a big event, or a little event that feels big.

Step 1: Have a comfortable seat. Roll your shoulders back and open up your chest.

Step 2: Set your left hand down gently and raise your right hand.

Step 3: Place your index finger on the spot in the middle of your forehead between your eyebrows. Start inhaling and exhaling through your nose.

Step 4: Use your thumb to close the right nostril and inhale through your left nostril.

Step 5: Now plug your nose with your thumb and middle finger like you're about to dive into a pool and hold your breath for a few seconds.

Step 6: Now lift your thumb off your right nostril and exhale until all air is out.

Repeat 10 times

Exercise: Box Breathing

Box breathing is another fantastic breathing exercise—and the best part is that you can do it anywhere. It distracts your mind as you're counting, soothes your nervous system, and lowers stress levels in your body. You can draw or visualize an imaginary box before starting as you will be tracing the lines as you're breathing.

Step 1: Count to four as you slowly exhale.

Step 2: Hold your lungs empty for another four-count.

Step 3: Then, take four counts to inhale.

Step 4: Finally, hold the air in your lungs for another count of four before repeating.

Exercise: Breath Focus

Breath focus is a simple but mighty breathing technique. If you can find a private place to recoup for a moment, this one can be extra effective—but you can still do it minus the verbal sighs if you're around other people.

Step 1: Breathe in and simply notice your breath. Where do you feel it? Do you feel it coming in through your nostrils? Perhaps you notice the rise and fall of your chest or abdomen?

Step 2: Let out a few sighs as you exhale. If that feels awkward, then form words like "calm," "safe," or "soothe." You can even swap out those words for funny words like "soup."

Step 3: Notice where you feel the breath as you exhale. Do you feel your lungs emptying out? Is your chest falling? Is air coming out of your nostrils?

Step 4: Repeat and see if you can notice small differences across your body each time.

Rate how you feel after completing this section.

Smooth Sailing (No Anxiety)	Don't Love It (Some Anxiety)	Hate It (More Anxiety)	NOPE NOPE NOPE (High Anxiety)
0	1	2	3

Getting Grounded (Not the Same as When You're In Trouble, Promise!)

Before you skip over this part and run for the hills, we're not talking about having all your electronics and privileges revoked, so don't panic!

Grounding techniques are simple brain exercises and mental games that help you focus on the present moment and connect with your surroundings. They involve focusing on what's happening around you and taking advantage of your senses to root yourself in present reality.

Why is it important to be in the moment? Well, when you're anxious, you're rarely in the moment. Your thoughts are almost always somewhere else. It's like being in a movie that's playing scenes in the wrong order—you experience flashbacks from old memories, or you picture stressful scenes that haven't even happened yet.

Grounding Exercises

Rate how you feel before starting this section.

Smooth Sailing (No Anxiety)	Don't Love It (Some Anxiety)	Hate It (More Anxiety)	NOPE NOPE NOPE (High Anxiety)
0	1	2	3

By forgetting the "then and there," and enjoying the "here and now," you're able to be fully present with your mind and chase off bothersome memories or fortune-telling visions. You can think through the situation logically rather than react emotionally, and as such, get your brain to realize that you're not in any real danger. As a result, your mind relaxes, your body relaxes, and you feel more empowered and in control.

Here are a few grounding techniques that you can try next time you're feeling anxious:

Exercise: 5, 4, 3, 2, 1

If you can count down from five, you can use this strategy to self-soothe when you're feeling anxious. You can use this one to bring yourself back to the present moment whenever you start feeling overwhelmed by your negative thoughts.

Step 1: Take a moment to see, hear, smell, taste, and feel what is happening around you.

Step 2: Identify 5 things you see around you, and say them out loud. "I see a fluffy dog."

Step 3: Identify 4 things you can feel, and say them out loud. "I feel the itchy socks my grandma knitted last Christmas."

Step 4: Identify 3 things you can hear. Say 'em out loud. "I hear the old lady next door singing opera."

Step 5: Identify 2 things you can smell. You know the drill—say them out loud. "I smell my gym bag on the other side of the room."

Step 6: Identify 1 thing you can taste, and say it out loud. "I taste a hint of hot cocoa left on my tongue."

Exercise: Soothing With the Senses

With so much information about the environment around you coming to your brain, it's no wonder your brain gets overwhelmed sometimes! Most of the information your brain processes are visual.

This activity helps activate some of your other senses to give your brain a break and help you move through distressing thoughts and feelings. This method is best used when you have some time and space to excuse yourself from a situation.

Step 1: Stimulate your sense of touch. You can do this by:
- Dipping your hands in water. How does it feel on your fingertips, palms, and knuckles? Start with warm water and then switch to cold. Which one feels nicer? Why? What did it feel like to switch temperatures?
- Grabbing any object near you. Is it warm or cold? Soft or hard? Smooth or bumpy? Think of as many adjectives as you can to describe how it feels.
- Focusing on the clothes you have on your body from head to toe. Which item feels heaviest? Lightest? Do the clothes feel smooth or scratchy?

Step 2: Stimulate your sense of smell. You can do this by:
- Heading outside. What does the air smell like? If there are plants, trees, flowers, or grass, take a moment to sniff them. Are the smells sweet or harsh? What do they smell like?

o   Going to the kitchen. Grab a piece of fruit or a vegetable from the fridge. Does it smell sweet or savory? How does it compare to other smells in your kitchen? Head to the spice cabinet. Go nuts smelling all the spices.

Step 3: Stimulate your sense of hearing. You can do this by:

o   Heading outside again. See if you can pinpoint 4-5 different sounds. Start by listening for things that are close to you and then start listening for things further away.

o   Taking a walk. Imagine the soundscape of your walk shifting as you go. Are things getting louder or quieter? Do you hear more natural sounds (birds chirping, wind blowing) or more urban sounds (cars going by, construction)?

Exercise: Categories

You can play this game anywhere, anytime, with just yourself or with others. It's a quick, fun, effective way to shift from anxious thinking to being in the present moment.

Step 1: Choose a category—can be something you know a lot or a little about. Examples might include ice cream flavors, musical artists, cute animals, or words in other languages.

Step 2: For 60 seconds, see how many things you can name in that category. You can write them down, make a mental list, or say them out loud.

Step 3: Pick another category and repeat.

Rate how you feel after completing this section.

Smooth Sailing	Don't Love It	Hate It	NOPE NOPE NOPE
(No Anxiety)	(Some Anxiety)	(More Anxiety)	(High Anxiety)
0	1	2	3

Visualization and the Power of Imagination

Have you ever entered a social situation having thought about all the ways it could go wrong?

When you're suffering from social anxiety, it's common to psych yourself out by picturing worst-case scenarios. But you're self-sabotaging with these visions!

When your brain has no other input besides real or imagined negative scenarios, it becomes convinced that you're in danger. That's when it starts the protection process that kept our caveman ancestors alive—heightened feelings of anxiety in preparation for full-on fight, flight, or freeze mode.

For example, when Isa thought about shooting free throws in front of Chloe's friends, she had the negative thought, "I will miss every single shot" pop into her head. Just thinking about missing a shot in front of Chloe's friends activated her sympathetic nervous system and her brain told her to high-tail it out of there.

Or take Jeremy's situation—the entire time he worked on his presentation, he visualized himself forgetting what to say while the class laughed at him. So by the time he got in front of the class, his nervous system was already primed for fight, flight, or freeze, leading Jeremy to experience real feelings of panic.

CHAPTER 3: CALM YOUR BODY

But by harnessing the powerful visualization process for calming your nerves instead of heightening them, you can control negative thoughts long before they control you. It's all about learning to control what kind of picture you allow your imagination to create.

Visualization Exercises

Rate how you feel before completing this section.

Smooth Sailing (No Anxiety)	Don't Love It (Some Anxiety)	Hate It (More Anxiety)	NOPE NOPE NOPE (High Anxiety)
0	1	2	3

There are many visualization exercises that can help you keep the uncomfortable symptoms of social anxiety under control. Here are some of the most effective visualization exercises for calming your nerves:

Exercise: Visualize Vanishing Anxiety

This exercise defies the rules of physics! You'll imagine transforming your anxiety into a real object that you can control in your mind. Find a comfortable, quiet place to sit down and follow these steps.

Step 1: Take a deep breath from your nose and let go of a big exhale from your mouth. Repeat three times, stretching each breath for as long as you can.

Step 2: Close your eyes and feel gravity press your body weight against the ground beneath you.

Step 3: Awaken your imagination to transform your anxiety into a physical object that will disappear. You control everything from the setting to the rules of reality. Here are some examples of vanishing visualizations you can try:

- Close your eyes and cup your hands as though you're holding liquid. Imagine your anxiety pouring from your head into your hands, your body feeling lighter as the heavy thoughts leave your body. When they feel "full," picture the liquid turning to tiny gas particles and floating away, leaving your hands empty again.

- Lie down somewhere warm and comfortable. Imagine yourself lying out on a beach under the sun. You're soaking in warm rays from the sun, and you're safe and happy. The longer you lie out in the sun, the more heat you build, melting the anxiety right out of your mind and body.

- Close your eyes and picture a gentle waterfall pouring into a crystal-clear pond. Imagine you're standing at the edge of the pond, dipping a toe into the cool, refreshing water. As soon as your skin touches the water, you feel the tension and anxiety tries to escape up your heel, into your calves. So, you dip both feet into the pond until you're hip deep in the water, wading towards the waterfall. The crisp, restoring waters pour over your head, drowning your anxiety and washing it away.

Exercise: Visualize Your Happy Place

Remember when you tricked your brain into making your mouth salivate for tacos? This activity is kind of like that, except you're convincing your brain into thinking you're in a serene, safe space so you can calm your anxious thoughts down.

Step 1: Sit in a comfortable position and take a few deep breaths.

Step 2: Close your eyes and bring awareness to your body. Slowly scan your body for tension and begin to release it from head to toe.

Step 3: Visualize yourself being transported somewhere else. Here is an example visualization you can try:

- Imagine yourself driving to the airport and hopping on a plane to a tropical paradise. As you get off the plane, feel the change in air from cool to warm. Picture the smells and sounds of the nearby oceanside and imagine yourself heading straight for the beach.
- Once you arrive, paint a vivid picture for your senses. Visualize the sound of the ocean gently crashing to shore, the smell of the salty air, the wind blowing the palm tree leaves around you, and warm sand beneath your feet.
- Next time you do a visualization exercise, you can swap the beach for another place you love.

Exercise: Visualize Anxiety as Your Spirit Animal

Showing compassion and acceptance of your anxious thoughts may seem strange, but you might be surprised at how empowering it can feel. This visualization exercise allows you to soothe your brain as you envision comforting your anxious spirit animal.

Step 1: Ponder over what your spirit animal looks like and allow it to take form. It may take the shape of your favorite animal, an animal you see frequently, or a beloved pet.

Step 2: Imagine the animal is upset and looks to you to feel safe and comforted. Feel yourself swell with empathy as you reach out to give it a big hug. Cuddle it close and tell it everything will be okay.

Step 3: As you snuggle with your spirit animal, envision how its fur or skin feels in your hands. What sounds, smells, and movements can you add to the scene to bring it to life?

Step 4: Your soothing presence brings peace to your spirit animal, and you feel your mind becoming peaceful as well.

Challenge: Create Your Own Scenario

You can even create your own visualization scenario—the possibilities are endless. Write a visualization series that either helps your anxiety vanish or carries you away to a happy place. Give it a shot!

_____

_____

_____

_____

_____

_____

_____

_____

_____

_____

_____

Visualization Tips

- Set a time each day to practice calming visualization. It's a good idea to incorporate visualization into your regular meditation practice. Use a timer and gradually increase the time spent visualizing from 3 minutes to 10 minutes or more.
- Be sure to imagine as much sensory detail as you can. Think of what you can see, smell, feel, hear, and taste.
- It may help to light some candles or play music in the background to help you focus.
- Don't get discouraged if you find it challenging to develop a clear picture at first. Visualization takes a lot of imagination!

Rate how you feel after completing this section.

Smooth Sailing (No Anxiety)	Don't Love It (Some Anxiety)	Hate It (More Anxiety)	NOPE NOPE NOPE (High Anxiety)
0	1	2	3

Progressive Muscle Relaxation

It's common to think of your mind and body as being separate. But you've probably noticed that your social anxiety leads to unpleasant feelings of tension and stress in your body—and vice versa. Maybe you've noticed that when you're in a social situation, your body seems to have a mind of its own. Your eye may twitch or your shoulders may bunch up around your ears without you even realizing it.

That's because high stress levels cause your brain to go into "protection mode" and your nerves tell your muscles to tighten. In the caveman days, this reflex made the body more resilient to attack.

You can see this evolutionary instinct in boxing or other fighting sports today. Fighters flex their abs and shoulders before anticipating an attack to help minimize the impact of the hit. That's exactly what your brain does to your body when you feel anxious—it tells your body to prepare for an attack to protect you.

Enter progressive muscle relaxation, which helps reverse this whole caveman survival instinct! It allows for increased blood flow and a release of all your muscle tension, alleviating stressful thoughts and promoting a sense of calm.

You'll like this one because it has an immediate effect that makes heaviness turn into weightlessness in your body, promoting relaxation and allowing your body to return to its base state of function. Progressive muscle relaxation is a powerful way of suppressing your body's sympathetic nervous response [fight, flight, or freeze] and activating your parasympathetic nervous system [rest and digest] instead.

What's cool about PMR is that it doesn't take long to complete. As you become better at PMR, you may become more aware of the places you tend to carry tension. For example, the jaw, eyebrows and shoulder muscles are very common places to experience anxiety. So when you begin to notice tension, you can make a conscious effort to relax your muscles.

Rate how you feel before starting this section.

Smooth Sailing (No Anxiety)	Don't Love It (Some Anxiety)	Hate It (More Anxiety)	NOPE NOPE NOPE (High Anxiety)
0	1	2	3

Exercise: Progressive Muscle Relaxation Exercise

The goal of progressive muscle relaxation (PMR) is to relieve the muscle tension associated with anxiety. By shifting your attention away from your thoughts and focusing on where you feel them, you can regain control of your body and clear your mind.

Step 1: To begin, find a comfortable place to sit or lie down. Then, close your eyes and bring your attention to your breath.

Step 2: Starting with your toes, tense the muscles in your feet for 15 seconds. Then, relax. Notice the change in sensation from tensing to relaxing your muscles.

Step 3: Then, move on your calves. Tense the muscles in the back of your calves by flexing as hard as you can. Let go and think about the change from tensing to relaxing.

Step 4: Now do the same with your thighs. Squeeze your upper thighs tightly and hold for 15 seconds. How do they feel? Release and note any change in sensation.

Step 5: Move on to your abdomen. Flex your abs hard and hold them for 15 seconds. Now, let them go. Do you notice any change to how your abdomen feels?

Step 6: Focus on your chest and shoulders. Squeeze your upper body muscles for 15 seconds. When you let them go, notice the differences in how your body feels.

Step 7: Shift down to your fingers. Make a tight fist, flexing finger and wrist muscles. After 15 seconds, slowly open your palms and relax your fingers. How does that feel?

Step 8: Move to your jaw muscles. Many people naturally carry a lot of tension in their jaws, so notice how different it feels to flex and relax these muscles for 15 seconds.

Step 9: Finish with your eyebrows. Flex your brow muscles by furrowing your eyebrows into an angry face. Hold and release, feeling the small muscles of your cheeks and forehead release, too.

Step 10: Take your time with your PMR exercises, allowing yourself time to experience the full cycle of tension and relaxation. Repeat a few times until you start calming down.

Rate how you feel after completing this section.

Smooth Sailing (No Anxiety)	Don't Love It (Some Anxiety)	Hate It (More Anxiety)	NOPE NOPE NOPE (High Anxiety)
0	1	2	3

Panic Attacks

During a panic attack, many people feel as though they're having a heart attack, or they're about to die. But you can go ahead and let out a HUGE sigh of relief because panic attacks aren't deadly, and you can learn to better control them with some of the techniques you've learned in this chapter.

This section will discuss what causes panic attacks, how to recognize them, and how to respond if you experience one. By having a plan in mind, you'll feel more prepared and confident to manage the feelings and sensations that lead to panic attacks.

What are Panic Attacks, and Why do they Happen?

A panic attack is a sudden, intense feeling of heightened anxiety that triggers a severe physical response. It can come on with no warning and usually lasts for several minutes. During a panic attack, you may feel heart palpitations, shortness of breath, sweating, nausea, and muscle pain in your shoulders, back, and chest.

Sounds like the typical anxiety symptoms, right?

Well, yes and no.

Panic attacks might come with your expected anxiety symptoms but at a more extreme level, and they often come with intense hyperventilation and dizziness.

The most common sign of a panic attack is feeling suddenly afraid or flooded with negative emotions; it may feel as if the walls are closing in.

No, having occasional panic attacks doesn't mean you're weird. On the contrary, many with SAD experience them. Panic attacks can feel random, but they always have a trigger. As you become more aware of your triggers, you can better prepare for, manage, and possibly reduce panic attacks.

Reframing Panic Attacks

If you're prone to panic attacks, taking some preventative steps is essential. One way to do this is to reframe your thoughts. This means that you change the way you think about a situation so that you're less likely to experience the flood of a panic attack.

When you feel the symptoms of a panic attack coming on, your instinct is probably to fight it off tooth and nail. But that won't serve you. Instead, as soon as you notice the symptoms coming on, accept them and your anxiety will begin to decrease. You'll eventually start building a tolerance for panic attacks.

You can usually tell when a panic attack is coming, and that's the part that feels so scary. You fear a problem that hasn't even become a problem yet!

Some common things you might say before a panic attack include:

- "I'm feeling lightheaded and dizzy. I'm afraid I might faint."

- "My face is starting to feel red—what if people see me with a beet face?"

- "I can't let this happen right now."

So rather than panic about what's going to happen, try to talk to yourself in a more positive and realistic way:

- "What do I need in this moment?"

- "I know this panic attack will only last a few minutes and then it will go away."

- "I accept this is happening and it won't last forever."

Exercise: Panic Attack Cheat Sheet

When experiencing a panic attack, it can be challenging to know how to calm down. The suggestions on this sheet aren't meant to teach you to fight panic attacks but, rather, to help self-soothe when they happen.

Acknowledge the panic attack. Accept that the panic attack is coming and focus on keeping control over your breathing. Remain where you are rather than trying to escape the situation and remind yourself that it's just your brain trying to protect you.

Activate calming techniques. This is where you can regain control and remind your brain that it's a false alarm, you're not in real danger.

Take Slow, deep breaths. Take deep slow breath through your nose until your lungs are full. Hold it for a few seconds. Then, take a long exhale from your mouth until your lungs are empty.

If you find yourself thinking about the panic attack, just gently bring your attention back to your breath and pay attention to what's happening in your body as you're breathing. Keep doing this every time your mind starts to panic.

Ground yourself. Latch onto your senses to keep yourself in the present moment. Pick one of the options below to quickly ground yourself:

- What do you see, hear, smell, taste, and feel? What do your clothes feel like on your skin? What does the ground feel like beneath you?
- If you're home, grab an ice cube and run it along your face and forearms or immerse your face in cold water to slow your heart rate. This works like magic!
- Chew gum. Science shows that chewing gum reduces anxiety by lowering the activation of our Fight-or-Flight response and decreases muscle tension.
- Look for objects around you and begin naming and describing them in your mind. I see a short desk lamp. I see my white shoes.
- If you can, take off your shoes and feel your feet touching the ground. This is called earthing and it helps you feel grounded, centered and in the present.

Repeat a mantra. A mantra is a word, phrase, or sound that gives you strength and brings your thoughts back to reality. Even simple phrases can do wonders to help you focus and slow your breathing. Some easy ones include:

- *This is going away soon.*
- *I'm calming down.*
- *Breathing is helping.*
- *It's almost over.*
- *I'm okay!*

The End of Chapter 3

If you were a video game character, you'd be strapped with every power-up, weapon, and secret cheat code you could ever ask for. By finishing this chapter, you've learned TONS of new tricks and hacks for managing the physical symptoms of SAD and calming your body.

The last thing to do is wrap up the experiment we began at the beginning of the chapter. Using the anxiety measurement charts at the beginning and end of each section, see if there's one that demonstrates a big difference.

Which one worked the best? Which one had the biggest impact on your body?

Store that one away to use for infinity—you can now use that technique forever and it will never deplete or wear out. In fact, the more you practice it, the better you'll become at it.

What are some words you would use to describe how you're feeling now? You're armed with tons of new self-soothing techniques to calm your body, so perhaps you're feeling confident and well-prepared. You know which calming techniques work best for your body, putting you that much more in control of your SAD symptoms.

Let's get a fist bump for that!

See you in chapter 4 for an even more powerful technique when you're ready.

CHAPTER 4

Embrace The Suck

Isa Takes a Risk

As Isa trudged towards school, her mind incessantly looped the wretched scene at the ice cream store. A lingering pang of guilt gnawed at her, knowing she had hastily abandoned Chloe. But her anxiety had spiraled to such dizzying heights that enduring the situation any longer had become unbearable.

When the bell rang for lunch that day, Isa headed to the library to hide out. She wasn't looking forward to seeing old Mrs. Cranklebee's unpleasant scowl when she walked in, but she was grateful for the escape the library provided all the same.

Except this time, she saw something she didn't expect. Chloe was waiting for her outside the library door.

Isa thought about making a run for it, but once their eyes met, she knew there was no turning back.

"Hey, Isa," Chloe said, a bit less cheerfully than usual. "Listen, is everything okay? I was worried when you left yesterday."

Isa sighed. She decided to be honest and said, "I felt really nervous when all those people came into the shop. I feel really—uh, *awkward* around new people."

Chloe began slowly, "I understand how you feel. I was going to ask if you wanted to join my group for the homecoming dance, but I guess you probably don't want to since ..." Chloe trailed off and looked at the ground.

Isa had completely forgotten about the homecoming dance. But the thought of disappointing Chloe again made her feel even worse than the thought of going to a dreaded school dance.

"Well, no, I ... it's just ..." Isa stammered.

"How about this?" Chloe asked, perking up.

"Why don't you just come and meet the group I'm going with, and maybe sit with us at lunch? If you hate it, you don't have to come, and I won't be mad."

Isa thought about it for a moment, and Chloe jumped at the opportunity to convince her.

"But Isa, I really think you would like the friends I've made so far this year. Will you just say hi to everyone? It's not as scary as it sounds, I promise!"

After a few moments, Isa nodded. She wanted to make it up to Chloe, and she had to admit, just saying hello didn't sound all *that* bad compared to spending yet another day with the meanest librarian in town.

And she could always bail from the cafeteria if things didn't go well. Summoning all of her courage, Isa trailed behind Chloe as they entered the bustling cafeteria.

The air seemed thick with tension, but Isa was determined to face her fears head-on. Chloe led her to a table where the group was waiting. With trembling hands, Isa mustered a shy wave for each girl.

"Hey, I know you. Lisa, right?"

It was Marcy, the girl she'd met in line waiting for her schedule. Isa almost said, *Yep, that's me, I'm Lisa.*

"No silly, it's *Isa*," Chloe corrected her.

Isa's stomach did a triple axel with embarrassment.

"Oh, sorry about that, I must have misheard you last time."

An apology? Isa hadn't been expecting that. Maybe these girls weren't so terrible after all?

After ten minutes of listening to the other girls chatter, Isa felt like she'd given it her all and felt ready to retreat.

"I'm just gonna go finish some homework, nice to meet you all," Isa told the group as she stood up to leave.

Marcy smiled at Isa and said, "Isa-Lisa, you should sit with us again tomorrow."

Isa took a deep breath as she considered. It hadn't been *that* bad, so maybe she wouldn't mind sitting with them again... just one more time.

"Okay, sure," Isa said, and waved goodbye as she headed back to the library.

Part of her was glad to be away from the overwhelming cafeteria, and part of her was sorry to leave, as the look on Mrs. Cranklebee's face when she came into the library revealed her to be in a particularly nasty mood that day.

I did it, Isa thought to herself and smiled as she closed the library door as silently as she could.

"Don't you slam that door, young lady!"

"Sorry," Isa said, still grinning from her triumph.

The next day, instead of heading straight to the library at lunch time, Isa headed to the cafeteria with the rest of her class.

Find someone else to yell at today, Isa imagined herself saying to grumpy old Cranklebee.

This time, Isa planned to try to stick it out at the lunch table for as long as she could. She grabbed her lunch, psyched herself up, and headed to the table with Chloe and Marcy.

"Oh, hey Isa, I was hoping you'd come sit with us again," Marcy said brightly.

She remembered my name!

"I don't have as much homework today," Isa explained.

"Are you coming with us to the homecoming dance?" Chloe asked.

Marcy and Chloe both looked at Isa hopefully.

Uh oh.

It was one thing to meet new people and sit with them at lunch. But going to a dance was a completely different story, and Isa still wasn't so sure how she felt about it.

"I have an idea," Marcy jumped in, glancing hopefully at Chloe.

"Why don't we do a little dress rehearsal before the dance? That way you can see how amazing you feel when you're all dressed up," Marcy grinned.

Isa had a feeling they'd planned what they were going to say if she didn't accept right away.

Chloe told her I feel awkward around people, and Marcy probably thinks I'm a weirdo now.

"Let me think about it," said Isa nervously.

"Okay, you think about it and we'll see you tomorrow night to try on our dresses for homecoming. I have a blue dress from 8th grade formal that would look incredible on you if you want to try it on," Chloe said, and Isa nodded slowly.

Blue is technically my favorite color…

"Alright, I guess that's fine. But, one thing," Isa hesitated for a moment.

"Can we—would it be okay if—let's do it at my house? That way…" Isa stopped.

"You don't have to explain yourself," said Chloe quietly. "We can come over to your house. Say, tomorrow at seven?"

Isa nodded and smiled faintly. Like the skilled communicator she was, Chloe tactfully switched the subject to which classes they loved and hated so far.

When the bell rang for the end of lunch, Isa was shocked. She'd been enjoying her conversation with the group so much, she hadn't even noticed that 45 minutes had passed.

I guess that wasn't as bad as I thought it would be.

The next day at 7 o'clock, Isa opened her door to find Chloe and Marcy standing in front of her with big smiles on their faces and armfuls of sparkly fabric spilling out of their hands.

"We brought a few extra dresses just in case," Marcy said.

Oh boy, what if I look ugly in every single one of them?

Isa showed them upstairs to her room and they began to try on the dresses.

"Blue is for you," Chloe exclaimed, handing a gorgeous blue dress glimmering with sequins over to Isa.

When it was her turn to try on a gown, Isa headed to the bathroom and closed the door. She carefully unzipped the dress and slipped it over her hips, and right away, she noted that it fit her like a glove. She'd never worn anything so glitzy and glam in her life, and it was only with much encouragement that Chloe and Marcy talked her into coming out of the bathroom to show them how she looked.

"Isa, you have to wear that dress, it looks amazing," Marcy declared, when Isa finally agreed to come out of the bathroom and show them how she looked in the blue dress. Chloe nodded emphatically in agreement, and Isa turned to glance at herself in the mirror.

She didn't usually like how she looked, but she had to agree—blue was definitely her color!

"Ew, what on earth are you wearing?"

Noah had poked his head out of his bedroom door down the hall.

"Oh hush, go back to your dumb video games," Isa said to Noah, surprised by her own confidence. Noah raised his eyebrows and retreated back into his room, closing the door with as much of a slam as he dared. Chloe and Marcy began laughing, and then Isa couldn't help but laugh, too.

Did I just do something funny? Am I actually funny?

"That's little brother speak for 'you look pretty.' My little brother is the same way," Marcy said as they recovered from their fit of laughter.

Isa agreed to wear the dress for homecoming, but deep down, she *still* wasn't so sure she actually wanted to go. Sure, she had managed to sit with new people at lunch, and even talk to a new friend like Marcy. But a *school dance*?

The thought still made her sick to her stomach.

As her friends headed home, Isa smiled and waved goodbye.

"No turning back now, you're coming with us. We're the three amigas now," Chloe called as they headed out the door.

No turning back...

She had faced her fear of sitting with new people at lunch—could she face her fear of the school dance, too?

Jeremy's Redo

When the last bell of the day rang to signal dismissal, the other kids filed out of the classroom and headed home without a care in the world.

But not Jeremy. He still had to redo his presentation for Mr. Garcia's class. And he was not looking forward to it *one bit.*

He slowly made his way back to Mr. Garcia's classroom. It would be awkward having to redo the presentation for just the teacher, but at least he wouldn't have to do it in front of the whole class.

When he opened the door to the classroom, his heart sank.

Apparently, a few other kids had messed up their About Me presentations too, because Jeremy saw several other miserable faces looking back at him.

"Looks like this is everyone," Mr. Garcia said, motioning for Jeremy to take his seat.

Jeremy hesitated, his eyes widening as Mr. Garcia pointed to a desk conveniently located right next to none other than Shania. He couldn't help but wonder if fate was playing a cruel joke on him. Did he really have to endure the humiliation of sitting next to the cutest girl in school on top of everything else?

"Come on buddy, we don't have all day," Mr. Garcia encouraged.

Jeremy made his way slowly to the desk, avoiding Shania's gaze at all costs.

"So, you bombed your presentations on the first try," Mr. Garcia began, looking out at the small group of students before him.

"You're probably feeling pretty bad about yourself right now. You're probably feeling frustrated, or feeling like you want to give up. You're probably feeling like a real failure."

Geez, he's really rubbing it in!

"That's a good thing. You want to know why? Because failure is a sign that you're growing stronger. Every time you fail, you get one step closer to success. You see those lights above your head? Thomas Edison tried and failed 10,000 times before he succeeded at making the light bulb work."

Jeremy looked up from the floor and thought about what Mr. Garcia was saying. He had never thought about failure that way before, but he didn't know if he could survive failing at this presentation 9,999 more times.

Mr. Garcia continued, "So you're going to have another chance to show what you've learned since this morning. You'll have ten minutes to tweak your presentations and prepare. Then, you're going to try giving your presentations again. This time, you'll give them to a partner."

There were only two people near Jeremy to partner up with. On one side was Shania. On the other side was a boy Jeremy had never seen or talked to before. Jeremy knew right away who he wanted as his partner.

"Uh, hey," Jeremy whispered to the boy as he sat beside him before Shania had a chance to ask him to work with her. "Want to be partners for this thing?"

The boy shrugged and gave him a thumbs up.

"I'm Elijah, what's your name?"

"I'm Jeremy."

"What'd you do to screw up your presentation, Jeremy?" Elijah asked.

"Oh, uh—I kind of just, you know, forgot what to say," Jeremy said, blushing.

"Classic," Elijah said, smiling. "I decided to hide out in the bathroom the whole period so I didn't have to give one," he smirked.

Jeremy had to hand it to him—on the surface it didn't sound like a terrible idea. But Mr. Garcia seemed too sharp to let a trick like that slide in his class. Obviously it hadn't worked because Elijah was sitting here with the rest of them.

"I just hate this kind of stuff, it makes me nervous," Elijah went on.

"Yeah man," Jeremy agreed, "I know exactly what you mean."

Jeremy and Elijah continued to chat as they worked on their presentations. When it was time for them to present to one another, Elijah decided to go first.

Jeremy watched as Elijah pulled off his presentation flawlessly.

What could he have been so freaking nervous about? He was perfect!

When it was Jeremy's turn, he admittedly felt slightly more confident than earlier in the day. He knew there wasn't a classroom full of kids to judge him this time—it was just him and Elijah. When Jeremy finished his presentation, Elijah applauded enthusiastically and gave him a high-five. Jeremy felt his face flush, but couldn't help feeling proud of himself.

"Not bad, my dude, not bad."

Jeremy looked up to see Mr. Garcia smiling from his desk in the corner of the room.

"See? I told you failure is a sign of growth."

When it was finally time to head home and Jeremy began packing up his stuff, a voice caught him by surprise.

"Hey, are you Jeremy?"

Jeremy turned, his heart sinking like a stone in his chest, only to come face to face with his worst nightmare—Shania.

Nope, not me, see that guy there? That's the real Jeremy.

"Um, yeah," he replied.

"Hi, I'm Shania, remember me from Ashton's party?"

"Uh, hi."

Jeremy's face burned so hot he thought he might combust. So he turned to the door to make his escape before he could embarrass himself any more.

"Wait, Jeremy, I wanted to ask," Shania started. She giggled and hid her face in her hands.

Is she nervous, too?

"I wanted to see if you were going to homecoming?"

Jeremy stared at her. He hadn't thought about homecoming, but he felt pretty confident about his answer. Elijah and Mr. Garcia were the only other people left in the room, and they were both staring at him with interest to see what he would say.

"No, I don't think so."

Shania raised her eyebrows.

"Oh, okay then. Well, bye, I guess" and she hurried past Jeremy through the door.

"Ouch," Elijah chuckled.

"What was that all about?" Jeremy asked, bewildered.

"You don't know, my dude?" Elijah asked him, grinning.

"Uh, no?"

"Come on, read between the lines. She wanted you to ask her to the dance!"

Jeremy's mouth fell open in surprise. Suddenly, he felt his phone buzz to life in his pocket. He slipped the phone into hand to find a text from Ashton:

Hey Jeremy! Having some friends over before homecoming this weekend. Come hang?

Before he could reply, he felt it buzz again.

I might have a friend who needs a date, maybe you know her? Her name's Shania.

Jeremy couldn't believe his eyes. He needed to come up with something to say, but he didn't know where to start. Elijah clapped him on the back.

"Good luck, man, she was kinda cute. I'd accept if I were you. Let me know if you don't, maybe I'll ask her out instead," Elijah teased as he headed out the door.

The Danger of Avoidance

Can you imagine if people avoided everything that made them uncomfortable? Our yards would turn into jungles of overgrown weeds, our dishes would pile up to the ceiling, and our teeth would rot right out of our heads. Mowing the grass, cleaning the kitchen, and going to the dentist are all things people would prefer to avoid, but must do in order to be healthy and live a fulfilling life.

As you learned in Chapter 1, when it comes to anxiety, avoidance is often the first response. Our instincts are to avoid situations that make us anxious in order to reduce our feelings of discomfort, but this strategy only serves to make the fear stronger and maintain feelings of anxiety.

Each time you succeed in avoiding a situation that causes anxiety, your brain says, "Hurray, we avoided danger and will live to see another day!" But, ultimately, avoidance reinforces the idea that a situation is dangerous and keeps us stuck in the cycle of fearful thoughts and behaviors. And this is what we call the Anxiety-Avoidance cycle.

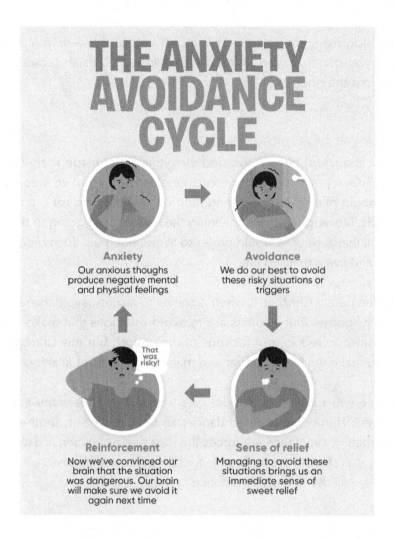

Exposure Therapy: Look Your Anxiety in the Eye

So how exactly are you supposed to convince your brain that you're actually not in any danger—especially when your SAD symptoms constantly make you feel like you're in danger?

You firmly stand your ground and prepare for a standoff. You take control of the way your brain responds to triggering situations using all the skills you've learned so far, and face them fearlessly!

Okay, maybe it's not that simple. But research has shown that facing your anxiety is the best way to gain control over your symptoms. This strategy is called exposure therapy and it's proven to be highly effective in treating the symptoms of SAD.

Exposure therapy works by slowly and gradually exposing you to the exact situation that causes your anxiety until your body physically stops responding with fear. And if you're shaking your head NOPE at the thought, just keep reading because it's not as bad as it sounds!

Exposure therapy isn't about diving into your anxieties head first. You don't have to perform a musical number in the middle of a party or lock yourself in a room with strangers to make it work. Go ahead, breathe a sigh of relief!

It's all about making progress one small step at a time. Don't worry too much about what to do right now—you'll learn lots of strategies to help you succeed throughout this chapter. We got you!

What Can Exposure Therapy Do For You?

So far, you've learned how to tackle two major links in the cycle of anxiety—your thinking patterns and physical responses. But your behavioral reactions to SAD are the largest, most important link of all.

By making yourself confront scary situations, you allow your nervous system to sort out its response to them. Exposure therapy allows you to "rewire" how your brain wants you to behave in triggering situations.

Over time, exposure therapy can:

- Reduce your sensitivity to SAD.
- Decrease your fear of social situations and performances.
- Improve your confidence around others.
- Empower you to enjoy a happy, healthy social life.

But It Sounds SCARY!

As terrifying as it sounds, facing fears head on has already proven to help millions of other people—and if you give it your all, it can help you, too! And just like you might be feeling nervous or scared to give exposure therapy a try, so did everyone else in the history of exposure therapy. It's okay to feel what you feel right now, just remember that lots of other people felt that way before they tried it, too.

Do you remember learning to ride a bicycle? Once those training wheels came off, you probably had a few wipe-outs (hopefully you were wearing a helmet and knee pads!) It was probably scary to get back behind the handlebars at first, but you overcame the fear and taught yourself to ride that darn bicycle a little better every day.

Exposure therapy works the same way—it's all about pushing yourself just a little bit outside of your comfort zone until eventually it feels like second nature. You'll have all your "protective gear" (the strategies you've learned so far) and start with "training wheels" on (you'll start small and ease into it a bit more each day).

See, it doesn't sound so impossible anymore.

Preparing for Exposure Therapy

The first step in exposure therapy is to reflect on the things that make you most uncomfortable, the situations that inspire the highest level of fear and anxiety. Thinking about the situations, your dread might make you feel uneasy, but it's important to work through this step, so you can best prepare to confront your fears.

To do this, you'll create your own **Fear Ladder.**

Fear ladders work almost like real ladders. They help you climb safely to the destination one small step at a time. The key is to know your

CHAPTER 4: EMBRACE THE SUCK

destination, or have an end goal in mind. To help you along your journey towards achieving your end goal, you'll use a fear ladder.

But, unlike real ladders, which all aim straight up and down, your SAD fear ladder will be completely unique from everyone else's. Why? Because the path you take to achieving your ultimate goal belongs to you and only you. You are the "builder" of your own ladder, the "researcher" of your own experience as you climb towards your goal.

Imagine the rungs of your ladder as small "experiments" that will help direct you towards your ultimate goal. You'll make a hypothesis about what you think will happen in each situation and compare it with what actually happens to see what you learn.

Example of SAD Fear Ladder

In the following fear ladder example, you'll see that there are a few different important sections:

- **Goal:** The ultimate thing you hope to achieve through exposure therapy.
- **Pre-Experiment:** You'll fill this section out before you start each challenge:
  - **Challenge:** These are the "rungs" of your ladder that bring you closer to the goal.
  - **Anxiety level:** This is where you'll rate the extremity of your anxiety when you think about completing the challenge.
  - **I'm worried that:** Explain what makes you feel anxious—what are you afraid will happen?
- **Post-Experiment:** You'll fill this section out after you complete each challenge:
  - **Rate actual anxiety level:** This is where you'll record the real level of anxiety you experienced while completing the challenge.
  - **The outcome:** Here, you'll record what the experiment taught you—was it different than you expected? What did you learn?

Note that the ladder should be read bottom to top, just as you climb a ladder.

ISA'S FEAR LADDER

My Goal:	Pre-Experiment			Post-Experiment	
Interact socially with my classmates	Challenge	Anxiety level	I'm worried that...	Actual-anxiety Level	Outcome
Step 10	Go to the dance with Chloe & the rest of the girls	9	My anxiety will show & they will laugh at m	TBD	TBD
Step 9	Do a dress rehearsal with Chloe & Marcy	7	I'll look ugly & awkward	7	I enjoyed dressing up with the girls
Step 8	Ask the other girls in the group to connect on social media	6	They'll say no	6	They said yes & we've been having fun hatting
Step 7	Talk one on one with Marcy	6	We'll run out of things to say & I'll look boring	6	There was an awkward silence, but we had a fun time
Step 6	Give someone a compliment at lunch	4	They'll think I'm being weird	4	Marcy was happy. People love compliments!
Step 5	Sit with the Chloe & her friends at lunch	5	I'll embarrass myself	5	I said something silly, but no one made fun of me
Step 4	Say hi to one of the other girls in the group	4	They won't want to talk to me	4	Marcy is nice & easier to talk to than I expected
Step 3	Meet the girls in the group	4	They won't like me	4	We have some things in common!
Step 2	Talk to Chloe about what going to the dance would be like	3	I don't want Chloe to know I'm nervous	3	Chloe is nervous too-I'm not the only one!
Step 1	Think about what going to the dance would be like	1	It's stressful to think about all the things that could go wrong	1	I can actually imagine things going well

Challenge: Build Your Own Fear Ladder

Carefully read the below steps before starting to
create your fear ladder.

Step 1: Create an ultimate goal.
Think of a goal you would like to achieve, something that is currently causing you difficulty. It could be as simple as attending a party or as difficult as giving an important presentation in front of your class. Choose something meaningful to you, so that you stay motivated to work towards achieving it.

Step 2: Break down your ladder "rungs."
You wouldn't expect a kid who just learned to ride a bike without training wheels to race a Formula One car, would you? Of course not. The same goes for exposure therapy—you'll want to make sure your rungs are within reach and realistic, in order to avoid potential setbacks.

Each step you take on the ladder leads to small, manageable moments of growth. These small mini-challenges might be broken down into 10, 15, or even 20 "rungs" in your fear ladder. As long as they aren't over-ambitious, you can't go wrong as you create your own unique rungs.

Step 3: Explain exactly what makes you uncomfortable.
For each rung on your exposure ladder, it's important to identify what thoughts, feelings, sensations, or images come to mind when you picture doing it. Are you afraid of being judged, or feeling humiliated, or having a panic attack?

Step 4: Rate each rung on the Fear Scale.

Use a fear scale (from 0-10) to rate the intensity of your fear for each step. If you notice large gaps between anxiety levels (a 3 next to a 7) break that rung into two so the exposure therapy feels more manageable.

You may need extra rungs on your ladder, or you may find you don't quite need all the rungs provided. Remember, you can take as many small steps as you need to reach your final goal. The key is stepping on the same "rung" as many times as necessary, until your anxiety reaches a point where you feel ready to move on to the next one.

Now, get started with creating your own fear ladder!

CLICK HERE OR SCAN

TO DOWNLOAD "MY FEAR LADDER" WORKSHEET

Psych Yourself Up for Exposure Therapy

Remember, each step along your ladder is an "experiment." As the researcher, you control the experiment and progress at your own pace. You get unlimited chances to succeed. It's not a test, there's no "right answer," and there's no deadline, so take all the time you need. You may feel challenged at times, but taking that first step forward is what matters most. The results matter less than the effort.

In time, your steady efforts will pay off (guaranteed!)—as long as you don't quit the experiment. When things get uncomfortable (and they will), know that your persistence is the key to progress. It's normal for your anxiety to worsen during exposure therapy—that means it's working!

But the sooner you can climb your ladder, the sooner your anxiety will melt away.

Hyping yourself up before taking the first step can make a big difference. Choose a motivational statement to help you power through when difficult times arise.

You might choose something like:

- *Anxiety sucks, but it's not dangerous.*
- *Bring. It. On.*
- *I'm feeling anxious, so what? I will live.*
- *If bad things happen, oh well—I'll find a way to cope.*
- *I'm in control, not my anxiety.*
- *One step at a time.*
- *I got this. I can do it. And if not, I will try again.*
- *It's only the first time that's the most difficult part. It will get easier.*

Pick Your Favorite Coping Strategies

We wouldn't make you go into your experiment without backup. Every scientist has their safety equipment, and you're no exception. You've already got a sizable "bag of tricks" to choose from when it comes to coping strategies that can calm your body and mind during moments of high anxiety.

Knowing which strategies work best for you is always a good idea when starting exposure therapy.

That way, you don't have to think about it—you'll have your plan ready to go in case things get tough.

Challenge: List Your Go-To Calming Strategies

Get ready to time travel ... back to chapter 3.

Highlight your favorite exercises from that chapter. Choose a few of these self-soothing techniques to store in your "back pocket" in case you become uncomfortably anxious in the middle of your exposure therapy experiments.

List your "back pocket" strategies below.

1. _____.
2. _____.
3. _____.
4. _____.
5. _____.
6. _____.

Practicing Exposure Before Doing It

Okay, are you ready to get the show on the road? Are your safety goggles strapped on tight? Do you have your lab coat buttoned up? Perfect—let's get started.

Exposure therapy begins with your imagination. In this stage, you'll visualize an anxious situation before actually doing any exposure. This visualization step is important because it helps you prepare to do it in real life. Visualization may reduce your anxiety, making the actual exposure easier.

Here's how it works:

Step 1: Set the scene by visualizing the details. Where are you? What do you see, hear, smell, feel, or taste? Who is there with you in the scene? What are you wearing? What are you feeling?

Step 2: If you get anxious during the visualization, take a moment to pause. Take some deep breaths, and then come back to it.

Step 3: Visualize yourself acting out the situation. What do you do? What do you say? What are some different ways others around you could react? How do you react to their reaction? Imagine as many different scenarios as you can think of.

If the visualization doesn't feel effective or doesn't seem to work on your first try, don't give up. Visualization is a skill which means you're totally able to get better at it with practice. Consistency is key!

Ready, Set, Go: The Rules of the Experiment

You've got everything you need to succeed in your experiment. Now, it's time to learn the rules of the game.

RULE #1 Stick it out as long as possible. Prolonged exposure (staying in an anxious moment until it feels mild) is incredibly effective, which is why it's so important to climb one tiny "rung" in your ladder at a time.

RULE #2 Practice makes perfect. Repetitive exposure (not stopping after just one exposure) is the key to climbing your ladder. Remember, you can repeat the same "rung" of your ladder over and over until it doesn't make you feel anxious (or only inspires mild anxiety).

RULE #3 No using safety behaviors. Safety behaviors take you back into your comfort zone. Since the whole point is to get you out of your comfort zone, there's no safety behaviors allowed (like looking at your phone to avoid talking, sitting in the corner by yourself, etc.).

RULE #4 Stay focused on your anxiety. Focus on staying in the moment with your anxiety. Rather than distracting yourself with a game on your phone or counting tiles on the ceiling, think about the way you feel in the moment. That way, you can retrain your brain to understand that there is no threat.

RULE #5 Move to the next rung of your ladder when it's time. Once the situation no longer gives you high anxiety, it's time to move to the next experiment. Make sure you keep the momentum going so you can continue the journey towards your goal.

RULE #6 Use your favorite coping strategies whenever you need them. Do whatever it takes to make the exposure last as long as possible.

What to Do When You Feel Anxious During an Experiment

Sometimes, even when you try your very best and use all the tricks you know to make it work, your anxiety level simply feels too high to continue. In that case, it's time to reboot with The Three Rs: Retreat, reset, and re-do.

- **Retreat** – remove yourself from the situation causing anxiety.
- **Reset** – allow yourself to recover and recharge and give yourself a pep talk as you prepare to try again—just don't wait too long (no more than a day).
- **Re-do** – give it another shot. Try using another calming technique or adding another rung to your fear ladder.

Here's the good news—this doesn't mean you failed. You get unlimited tries to get it right.

If you realize things don't feel easier after multiple attempts at one of the challenges, then it might be a good idea to revisit your fear ladder. Double-check that your steps are manageable and make adjustments if needed. Each step should feel a little bit more uncomfortable than the last, but don't try to push yourself too far.

For example, if Isa realized that sitting with the group at lunch felt too overwhelming, she might reassess the rungs in her ladder. Rather than going straight into the cafeteria and sitting at the table to socialize for the whole lunch period, she adds a step where she sits with them for the last ten minutes of lunch instead.

Feel free to go back and revise your ladder as needed so that it feels appropriately challenging and achievable.

After the Experiment: The 4 Rs

Reward: First things first—once you do something brave and push yourself outside of your comfort zone, it's time to celebrate! Reward yourself for what you were able to achieve by doing something you enjoy.

Rate: After you're done doing a happy dance, it's time to get back to the experiment. Return to the fear ladder and fill in the blank column "Actual Anxiety Level" in the post-experiment section.

- How do you feel post-exposure?
- Has your anxiety level improved?

Reflect: How did the actual experiment go compared to what you thought would happen? Go back to the fear ladder and add your thoughts to the blank column "Outcome" in the post-experiment section.

- Did the experiment go as you expected or did it go differently?
- Was there anything positive that came out of your experience?
- What did you learn about yourself in the process?

Repeat: It might seem silly to keep repeating the same challenge over and over, but it works! Keep repeating the challenge and recording your reflections until your anxiety feels milder. Then, you can move on to the next rung in your ladder. That way, your pace gives your brain time to "catch up" as it learns that you aren't in any real danger along the way.

Remember, there's no deadline, and it gets a little easier each time!

What If You Keep "Failing" at an Experiment?

It might happen—you might just keep retreating and recovering until you feel stuck on a single rung. Know that this is totally normal. It's normal to feel a strong sense of fear or hesitation, and it's normal to want to quit when you don't succeed after the first few tries.

But here's something that might surprise you—failure is a good thing! It means you're growing and learning. And it only gets better afterwards! If you didn't feel discomfort or if you mastered everything on the first try, your ladder wouldn't be needed in the first place.

Be okay with temporary failure—actually, be excited to fail because it means you're getting closer to success. If you never fail through the experiments, it's probably because the process isn't working the right way. Failure is a sign you're making change. We should actually celebrate failure as we do success!

Every successful person in the world has experienced failure before they experienced success because it's a natural part of the process. If they had let those failures stop them, they would have missed out on the chance to become who they are today. See failure as a good sign that you're on the right track.

There's no past version of yourself that's as strong as the person you are right now. Past failures don't mean future failures, especially considering you grow stronger after each failure. Allow your desire to succeed to be larger than your fear of failing again.

When Things Don't Go As Planned

Life is full of unexpected twists and turns, so don't panic when your attempts at each challenge don't go as planned. Here are some tips to keep you focused on the end game.

Acknowledge your emotions: It's normal to feel discouraged when you try something without success. Instead of avoiding or pushing away these feelings, acknowledge them and allow yourself to feel whatever comes up. Then, use your newfound understanding of how you feel to create a plan for how to move forward.

Be patient with yourself: Patience is key! It can take time to learn a new skill or break through your fear. There's no magic formula for success, so be kind to yourself and trust the process. Focus on the journey, not the destination.

Don't worry about what other people think: There's no one in the world who hasn't been embarrassed in front of people. Every human on the planet has their embarrassing moments, but here's the thing—even if you do something embarrassing, people will forget all about it sooner than you might think.

In fact, a Professor at Portland State University School of Business, Art Kohn, states that: "on average, 50% of new information is forgotten after one hour." So chances are, other people won't even remember your goofs the next time you see them!

Instead, use each experiment as an opportunity to cultivate self-awareness and learn more about yourself. Enjoy the journey and the successes along the way—you're in it for the long haul.

The End of Chapter 4

Avoiding anxiety-provoking situations is like building a fortress around yourself, keeping you trapped in a cycle of fear. But exposure therapy is like a courageous explorer, gradually venturing deeper into uncharted territory to conquer anxiety.

Think of exposure therapy as a personal trainer for your mind. Just as you would start with light weights and gradually work your way up, creating a fear ladder allows you to take small steps outside your comfort zone until you can conquer your anxiety with ease.

High five for finishing another chapter—see you in chapter 5 when you're ready to jump back into it!

How Exposure Works

NEW BELIEFS & EXPECTATIONS

You have now proved to your brain that saying "hello" to the person next to you is not a dangerous situation.

The next time you need to say "hello", your brain will put less effort into talking you out of it. Protection mode: off!

Congratulations, you have overcome your first fear! Now it's time to move to the next level and face another (temporarily) scary situation.

REDUCED ANXIETY

AHA!

Now, saying hello to the person next to you doesn't seem that catastrophic.

You've done this several times before and you didn't die. Also you know how to calm yourself if you got anxious.

USING COPING MECHANISM + REPEATING EXPERIMENT

Now it's time to use smoothing techniques to calm your body before and during the scary situation.

If the first try did not go well, you retreat from the mission, recover, and retry the same situation another another time.

Next, keep repeating the exact same exposure over and over again until the thought of it does not make you feel sick, and the situation only gives you a mild anxiety.

NEGATIVE THOUGHTS & INCREASED ANXIETY

The thought of doing that makes you feel too anxious (thinking about all the things that could go wrong, how you will be judged and embarrassed etc.).

These thoughts start making you feel negative emotions (fear, dread, anxiety) and physical symptoms (heart race, sweat, butterflies, nausea etc.).

FACING FEAR

Here You start to expose yourself to one scary situation at a time, starting from the least terrifying one and gradually moving up to scarier situations one by one.

For example, start with just saying "Hello" to the person next to you in class.

CHAPTER 5

The Significant Six

Isa and The Three Amigas

Isa watched the pendulum swinging back and forth on the old grandfather clock in her living room. Above it, the hands of the clock inched ever closer to 6 o'clock.

Chloe and Marcy would arrive to pick her up for the dance soon.

Isa glanced out the window and caught a glimpse of her reflection looking back at her. Why on earth did she let her mom talk her into curling her hair like that? She wound her finger around a stray ringlet and tucked it behind her ear. What if everyone thought she looked funny?

Isa breathed in deeply, looked away from her reflection, and tried to let the thought go.

"You gonna dance with someone tonight?"

Isa turned to see her little brother Noah attempting to spin a basketball on his fingertips as he walked into the room. He tucked the ball under her arm, and with a running start, hopped over the coffee table and into the armchair.

"If mom saw you do that you'd be toast. And I don't dance. I do dunk on little punks like you out on the court though," Isa teased.

"Only 'cuz you're older."

"And I'm better."

"No you're not. Bet you can't dunk on me in that dress!"

The doorbell rang, and Isa immediately found herself wishing she could just stay home and play ball with Noah—even if he was being the world's most annoying little brother.

"Have fun not dancing at the dance," Noah said with a smirk. "I'll be practicing outside." Isa wished she could follow him as he headed for the back door. Instead, she headed to the front door where her mother waited.

When she opened the door, Isa saw Chloe and Marcy waiting for her.

"Hi, Isa! Don't you look gorgeous," Chloe said as they came inside.

Isa felt her face burn hot with embarrassment.

"I'm so glad you agreed to go to the dance with us," Marcy said excitedly.

"Now we're like the Three Amigas," Chloe added.

But as they posed for pictures, Isa wasn't sure she was glad that she agreed to go to the dance. As much as she wanted to be part of the Three Amigas, she still doubted whether she was actually ready to take all these really big steps. Going to a school dance with hundreds of other kids, having to socialize with friends the entire night—everything felt like it was moving too fast.

Isa felt her heart start to race.

"Can you text those to me?" Chloe asked after Isa's mother finished snapping the pictures. As the others scrolled through the pictures, Isa glanced out the window and saw Noah dribbling lazily on the driveway.

She sighed and longed to join him.

"Everything okay?" Marcy asked.

Isa nodded, but Marcy knew better.

"I hear you're really good at basketball," she said. "Want to shoot some hoops really fast before we go?"

Isa stared at her in bewilderment.

"What do you—in heels and a dress?"

"Sure, might loosen up your nerves. I've heard exercise can do that!"

Marcy lifted the skirt of her long dress and headed for the door. Isa stood surprised for a moment before following her outside.

As she came around the corner to the driveway, she saw Noah pass the ball to Marcy. They laughed as she dribbled, shot, and missed.

"Come on, Isa, you really think you can dunk the ball in a dress?" Noah asked.

Isa thought about it for a moment before motioning for Marcy to pass her the ball. She dribbled for a moment and took a deep breath. Then, Isa rushed for the hoop, pushed the ball into the air and … swoosh. Score.

They played for a few more minutes before Marcy complained she was getting sweaty and called it quits.

"Time to party, let's go!" Chloe called a few minutes later, and Marcy and Isa headed back inside.

As she climbed into the car to head to the dance, Isa still felt a little nervous. But she had to admit she felt better. Maybe Marcy was right—maybe moving your body did help soothe your nerves.

Jeremy Lets Loose

Jeremy looked around and couldn't believe his eyes.

Somehow, he'd let Ashton talk him into going to the homecoming dance with his friends. The worst part? He'd been set up on a date with Shania.

Jeremy could barely look at her. She was buckled into the seat beside him as they headed to the dance in Ashton's mom's gigantic mini-van. It was hard not to look at her in that bright green dress with her long strawberry blonde hair pulled back into a neat braid.

A few times, the two had made eye contact. Once, he thought she was going to say something to him, so he panicked, took out his phone, and quickly looked away.

Jeremy had envisioned going on a date many times. But in his vision, his future-self knew how to talk to girls. He could easily make them laugh, or land a date to the movies if he wanted.

Now that he was sitting in the car next to a real live date, he wished he had practiced more lines, more jokes—anything so that Shania didn't think he was such a weirdo. But instead, he'd been up all night worrying about the dance, visualizing nearly every single way things could go sideways.

As the other kids in the car chatted excitedly, and sang along when their favorite songs came on, Jeremy yawned and shrunk back into his seat. The lack of sleep seemed to be creeping up on him.

"Jeremy?"

The sound of his name jolted him back awake. Stomach sinking, Jeremy turned to see Shania looking directly at him, smiling faintly.

"Do you maybe want to dance with me when we get there?"

"Uh, I'm not a great dancer," he said nervously.

"Me neither, but I don't mind if you don't," Shania laughed.

Jeremy couldn't think of what to say back. If he said he did mind that neither of them was any good at dancing, she'd think he was being a jerk. But if he said he didn't mind, then he'd be stuck on the dance floor making a fool of himself in front of the entire school.

So he nodded and looked back at his phone, hoping to find a way out of the situation before it came time for dancing.

Jeremy could hear music and as soon as they turned into the school parking lot. The music grew louder as they approached the building, accompanied by the sounds of laughter, singing, and cheerful voices.

As everyone else climbed out of the car first, a thought occurred to Jeremy—what if he just stayed here and asked Ashton's mom to take him home? He could say he wasn't feeling well, which wasn't exactly a lie.

"You coming, Jer?"

Ashton stood outside the car, holding the door open.

"Ah, I don't feel super well," Jeremy said quietly.

"Come on, you'll feel better once we get inside. I'm not letting you bail on me this time," Ashton said with a reassuring smile.

Jeremy stepped out of the car, took a deep breath, and braced himself for the inevitable awkwardness of the school dance. It was like walking into a lion's den, except instead of lions, there were sweaty teenagers swaying to the beat of Top 40 hits.

But hey, what's the worst that could happen? He could accidentally spill punch on himself, get rejected by his date, or trip and fall in front of everyone. At least he'd have a good story to tell.

What are The Significant Six?

You've probably envisioned a "future-you" at some point. You know, the future you who deals with SAD like a true boss and feels composed and confident around other people?

Imagine all the things you hope to be true for your future self. Maybe you want future-you to get good grades and have a few close friends. Or maybe you picture future-you like Jeremy does, making people laugh and landing a date to the movies once in a while.

Go ahead, imagine the smile on the face of future-you when you achieve those goals.

How exactly do you make this future-self come true?

Believe it or not, part of the answer lies in your day-to-day routine. As the old saying goes, you are the sum of your habits. In other words, to become the best version of yourself, you'll need to work towards that goal, little-by-little, each day.

And here's a fun fact for you: Your mind and body are like two peas in a pod. So even making small improvements to your daily habits can help you feel more confident and at ease.

The Significant Six

In this chapter, we'll look at six habits that researchers have found to improve social anxiety symptoms.

- Sleep
- Diet
- Exercise
- Acts of Kindness
- Journaling
- Mindfulness

Before we get started, remember this: changing your habits takes time and discipline. It doesn't happen overnight. So rather than trying to make drastic changes, the key is to focus on implementing new habits, one at a time, over the course of weeks and months.

Set realistic goals and allow yourself to feel proud of those positive changes, as you consider the Significant Six

The Importance of Getting Enough Zzzs

BREAKING NEWS: Teens need their beauty rest.

Do you dread the sound of your alarm in the morning? Besides the fact that your bed is probably the warmest, coziest place in your whole world, your body may be telling you it needs more deep sleep.

So what exactly is keeping you awake at night and preventing you from falling into a restful sleep? SAD could be to blame, as it tends to cause one or both of the following types of thoughts:

1. **Rumination:** Do you ever find yourself replaying past social scenarios that make you feel embarrassed over and over again? Maybe you find yourself overanalyzing social situations and picking apart your interactions with others. This is called rumination, and while everyone certainly does it at some point, people with SAD tend to take it to the extreme.
2. **Anticipatory processing:** When a stressful event looms on the horizon, you may find yourself in distress about all the things that could go wrong. That's when your brain looks into its magic crystal ball and starts predicting how terribly everything is sure to go—except crystal balls don't work, and things probably won't actually be that bad.

Keep in mind that it's totally okay to have these types of thoughts for a brief time. Even people who don't suffer from social anxiety have these kinds of thoughts.

But negative thought patterns are especially damaging for people living with SAD because they often fester out of control. As a result, they disrupt your ability to relax and fall asleep.

Did you know that sleepless nights can raise anxiety by up to 30%? Lack of sleep causes your body to produce more of the stress hormone called cortisol (sound familiar?). When your cortisol levels are too high, it affects your body's ability to get enough REM (rapid-eye movement) sleep, a type of deep sleep that makes your brain actively forget excess information to prevent the cognitive overload that makes people feel anxious.

When you don't have enough REM sleep, you'll wake up feeling tired, and you may experience side effects such as brain fog, loss of memory, and even paranoia.

No, thanks!

Remember how miserable Jeremy felt in the car on the way to the dance after staying up all night worrying? That's the kind of effect we're talking about here, and it does NOT sound fun!

It makes sense that Jeremy felt terrible after losing sleep. The more scientists learn about sleep, the more they uncover its importance to our overall health and wellbeing.

Research shows that adolescents and teens should be getting as many as nine or ten hours of sleep every night. With your mind and body developing at such a rapid pace, sleep gives your body a period of much-needed rest so it can carry out important functions.

For example, you need sleep to:

- Maintain a healthy body.
- Keep your immune system functioning.
- Maintain good mental health.
- Stay energized throughout the day.
- Store memories.

If you're feeling sleep-deprived, don't worry—we have some scientifically proven tips to help you get back on track.

Improving Sleep Hygiene for More Restful Sleep

Sleep has hygiene standards. That's right—just as you have to bathe and brush your teeth every day to maintain good physical hygiene, you need healthy routines to maintain good sleep hygiene. Sleep hygiene refers to your habits surrounding sleep, and it can be especially helpful for building up your "armor" against SAD.

- **Keep a consistent bedtime routine:** Bedtimes aren't just for little kids—big kids (including adults) benefit from getting to bed early, too! It takes a little discipline, but if you can manage to get to bed at a decent hour on weeknights, you'll be in good shape. And if you can maintain your schedule on weekends, even better!

  Start by getting ready for bed at around the same time every evening to help trigger your brain to produce melatonin, your body's sleep hormone. Take a bath, read a book, or listen to a podcast as you wind down for the evening.

  Just be sure to avoid scrolling on your phone about an hour before bedtime, as the blue light and stimulation of screens wreaks havoc on your sleep cycle. Exposure to blue light has a strong impact on your ability to fall asleep and stay asleep, so you won't be doing yourself any favors by doom scrolling.

- **Create a cozy bedroom environment:** Keeping a neat and comfortable room can be super effective in helping you fall into the deepest possible sleep. Tidy up, lower the lights, and listen to some soft music before hopping into bed. If you don't already, try making your bed and seeing how wonderful it feels to hop into a made bed in the evening (it's really one of life's small joys).

- **Avoid caffeine in the afternoons and evenings:** Caffeine has a half-life of about four to six hours. That means if you have coffee at 3pm, half of the caffeine could still be in your system at bedtime! Stick to non-caffeinated beverages later in the day to guarantee a better sleep.

- **Don't eat or drink too much before bedtime:** Big meals can make it hard to fall asleep because your body has to devote so much energy to the digestive process, putting your need for sleep at odds with your need for digestion. Similarly, drinking too much fluid before bed might make you wake up to go to the bathroom. If you're hungry after dinner, stick to a light, healthy snack such as fruit that won't overload your system.

- **Limit napping:** It's understandable to feel drowsy throughout the day, especially if your anxiety keeps you up at night. But napping can interfere with your sleep cycle, so it's best to avoid it if you can. If you must nap, set an alarm for 20 minutes, then hop out of bed and go for a walk to re-energize.

- **Get your body moving:** When it comes to sleep hygiene, exercise is your best friend. Try to get at least 30 minutes of physical activity each day and you'll find it much easier to fall asleep. Just make sure you're not exercising too close to bed-time, as that can make it hard for your body to wind down and fall asleep.

Hacks to help you fall asleep:

Exercise: Miliary Method: How Pilots Fall Asleep

The military method was developed by the Navy to help pilots fall asleep. Here's how it works:

Step 1: Relax your face. Close your eyes, breathe deeply, and allow all your facial muscles to relax, including your jaw and eyebrows.

Step 2: Relax your arms. Release any tension you're carrying in your hands, arms and shoulders.

Step 3: Relax your chest. If you're still holding tightness in your chest, exhale and feel the tension dissipate.

Step 4: Relax your legs. One by one, let your feet, calves, and thighs sink into the bed.

Step 5: Relax your mind. Focus on your breath. As thoughts pop up, simply notice them, and refocus your attention to your breath.

Exercise: Wind Down with Breathwork

For a simple breathing exercise, try counting each breath.

- Inhale: 1.

- Exhale: 2.

- Inhale: 3.

- Exhale: 4.

Keep counting with every inhale and exhale until you reach 10. Then start over at 1. Keep doing this to distract your mind and keep it focused on your breath until you drift off to sleep.

Tip: Read a book before Bed

Many find it easier to drift into sleep after reading a book. Even five or ten minutes of reading can distract you from anxious thoughts, reduce stress, allow your body and mind to relax enough to make you tired and fall asleep. A bonus: you might have more interesting dreams!

Tip: Wear Socks to Bed

In 2018, scientists decided to test out the old wives' tale that socks help you sleep better. Turns out, by keeping your feet just a couple of degrees warmer each night, you can fall asleep faster (to the tune of about seven minutes) and get an extra 30 minutes of sleep-in total. So, keep those tootsies warm!

Tip: Take a Warm Shower or Bath

One of the best ways to get your melatonin flowing is with warm water. In 2019, one study found that soaking for just ten minutes can improve your sleep quality compared to not soaking.

Tip: Indulge In a Small Bedtime Snack

If you're hungry before bed, try eating a banana, which has been shown to improve sleep quality. You may also try eating a small amount of other magnesium and potassium-rich foods, such as kiwi, walnuts, almonds, yogurt, and oats. Or, try drinking milk, chamomile tea, or tart cherry juice.

Nutrition: You Are What You Eat (Literally)

This is the second of the Significant Six habits to relieve anxiety, and it's all about Diet.

Weird as it may sound, your stomach is basically your second brain.

No, there's not a squishy ball of gray matter floating around in your gut like the brain inside your skull. But there are trillions of bacteria that live in your gut (called your gut microbiome) that can have a profound impact on your mental health.

As research uncovers more about the link between the gut and the brain, scientists are beginning to understand that food choices significantly impact our mood and thought patterns.

What goes in must come out—in more ways than one! An unbalanced diet can sabotage your gut microbiome, which is directly linked to cognitive issues. Over time, unchecked dietary transgressions lead to inflammation— one of the causes of many physical and emotional symptoms of anxiety.

But enough doom and gloom.

It's actually good news that you have a "second brain" because that means food isn't just for settling grumbling tummies—it can also be used as a medicine. Just like doctors prescribe medicine to heal illnesses, food can be a kind of preventative medicine that helps your body avoid trouble in the first place.

Superfoods That Are Like "Medicine" for SAD Symptoms

> ***One note before you read this section***
>
> Before you try any of the foods mentioned in this section, be sure to note any food allergies you might have. Don't try foods that may cause an allergic reaction.

Eating **superfoods,** or foods that have benefits due to their exceptional nutrient density, is a smart way to keep your second brain happy. No, we're not robbing you of your pizza or soda—so go ahead and breathe a big sigh of relief.

Instead, you'll learn about small foods and how you can include them easily in your diet. Just making a few small, healthy choices throughout the day will add up over time, especially as you grow to love some of these delicious superfoods.

Satisfy your sweet tooth:

- **Dark chocolate:** looking for a little pick-me-up? Reach for a dark chocolate bar. Dark chocolate contains substances that increase endorphins and make you feel happier. It's also full of antioxidants, so it packs a double punch!
- **Yogurt:** yogurt has beneficial probiotics, which helps keep the gut microbiome balanced. Studies have found that people without depression had significantly higher levels of beneficial bacteria in their gut than those WITH depression. Pro tip: yogurt is the perfect breakfast or dessert—just throw in some fruit and drizzle with honey.
- **Berries:** Strawberries, blueberries, and raspberries are all fantastic sources of antioxidants. Antioxidants help protect your cells from damage caused by free radicals, which can cause inflammation that contributes to depression and anxiety. Throw some berries into a smoothie or sprinkle on top of your favorite yogurt.

Savory superfood snacks:

- **Popcorn:** Popcorn is rich in magnesium, which helps regulate serotonin levels and promote better sleep. Also, it's a delicious snack that you know will serve your health—sounds like a win-win.

CHAPTER 5: THE SIGNIFICANT SIX

Pop your own at home on the stove, and sprinkle a little sea salt on top for a healthy mood-boosting snack.

- **Nuts:** Nuts are filled with omega-3 fatty acids which have been found to stabilize mood, reduce depression symptoms and promote a healthy brain. Keep a bag of nuts in your bag to nibble on when you feel snackish.

- **Eggs:** Eggs contain choline, which helps regulate hormones. They also have B6, folate and B12, which are all necessary for proper brain functioning. Trust and believe—making eggs a breakfast routine is a good idea.

More Super Nutrition Tips for Feeling Like Your Raddest Self

Now that you know which superfoods to add to your diet, here are a few other dietary tips to make the most of your "second brain":

- **Make H2O your best friend.** This is going to sound gross, but your body sweats a lot—up to a gallon or more on an average day. That means you have to make sure you drink lots of water from the moment you wake up in the morning.

  Chug water in the morning to get your organs moving and carry a water bottle with you to work or school. Aim to drink between 11 to 16 x 8 oz glasses of water per day.

- **Feed your brains breakfast.** Your skull brain and your stomach brain need nutrients to do their jobs. In fact, one study found that eating breakfast correlated to healthier habits, including eating more balanced macronutrients throughout the day.

  One study showed that breakfast-skippers were at a higher risk of experiencing stress, depression and psychological distress, in addition to anxiety in adolescents. So the moral of the story is simple—eat your dang breakfast!

- **Grandma was right—you've got to take your vitamins.** Build life-long healthy habits by taking a daily multivitamin. Consult your parents, doctor, or a nutritionist to find out which vitamins and minerals are right for you. Don't forget to add in omega-3s and probiotics to keep your brain and gut in balance.

- **Make easy swaps: Try this instead of that.** Limiting certain foods before social situations can help alleviate some of the anxiety they cause. Here are some easy swaps you can make to set yourself up for success:

Try this instead of that:

- **Drinks:** Drink chamomile or green tea instead of coffee.

- **Snacks:** Berries, walnuts, and popcorn instead of chips or crackers.

- **Bread:** Whole grain instead of white bread.

- **Dessert:** Dark chocolate or your favorite fruit instead of candies or lighter, sugary chocolates.

Keep focusing on making healthy choices one day at a time. And don't put too much pressure on yourself—get creative with incorporating these foods into your meals and snacks when you can and enjoy experimenting with your favorites.

Bon appetit!

Exercise: A Body In Motion Stays In Motion

Your body may be feeling the burn, but your brain gets a workout, too, when you get your sweat on. That's because exercise helps you practice mindfulness, or being in the moment, and it's the third in our list of Significant Six habits to help with anxiety.

Whether you're doing yoga, playing soccer, or learning a new dance, focusing on body movement helps you feel present and grounded in your body, giving your anxious thoughts a chance to rest.

Isa didn't know it at the time, but shooting hoops to calm her nerves before the dance was one of the best things she could do for herself. Instead of wasting energy panicking about all the things that could happen at the dance, her brain focused on the motor skills needed to dribble and shoot the basketball.

The physical activity caused her brain to release feel-good hormones like endorphins and dopamine, giving her a little boost of positive energy before heading to the dance.

It's well known that exercise lowers anxiety and increases confidence. The magic of exercise works like this: Physical activity reduces levels of cortisol (that nasty stress hormone we keep mentioning) and also releases endorphins, which provide sparks of energy.

Exercise Doesn't Have to Suck—Honestly

The thought of lifting massive weights or drowning in sweat as you climb a Stairmaster may send you running for the hills (hey, that's a workout too, right?).

But news flash: Exercise doesn't have to look like this—*it doesn't have to be a punishment!*

Find ways to move your body that you actually enjoy and look forward to. Maybe that means riding your bike on a trail or playing a video game with a dance mat. If you haven't found your "thing" yet, that's okay.

Try new things until you find an activity you enjoy. To start out, try doing something active for ten minutes a day and ramp up the intensity and frequency.

How to make your workouts more enjoyable:

- **Find a workout buddy.** Having someone to encourage you and talk to makes exercise much more fun.
- **Create a playlist with some of your favorite tunes.** Music can help you stay motivated and make the time go faster.
- **Aim for variety in your routine.** Exercise doesn't have to be the same thing every day! Try out different activities or switch up your routine for a change. Anything that moves your body and gets your heart rate up is good enough!
- **Be outside in nature.** In addition to all the physical health benefits. Exercising in nature makes us feel happier and more at peace because it provides a healthy outlet for negative thoughts and emotions and reduces cortisol. Bonus: exercising in fresh air is easier than indoors! Research has also suggested that just five minutes in nature is all it takes for our brain to start thinking differently and for us to relax.
- **When you feel ready, try a social fitness activity.** We get it—team sports might be hard, but once you're ready for the challenge, they're a solid way to practice social interactions while also working out your body and mind.
- **Track your exercises.** Get an app or fitness watch. Seeing your progress will give a feeling of accomplishment, which will increase your motivation to keep going!

Kick Negative Thoughts to the Curb

Getting yourself to engage in more movement can be a challenge, especially if you're not used to it. Your brain may naturally try to resist and try to talk you out of it when the time comes to start moving.

But you're too smart to fall for that—for every excuse your stubborn mind can come up with, you can also come up with a winning argument in favor of exercise. Remember, you don't have to believe the statements you're making to motivate yourself, just keep repeating them, and your brain, being the computer that it is, will start to accept and believe them over time.

Here are some of the most common excuses people use and some examples of thoughts to counter them.

- It's boring/I hate exercising → I'm excited to try something new and see if I like it.

- I'm exhausted/overwhelmed → Exercising will give me a much-needed mental break from the stress of this day.

- I'm hopeless/nothing can help me → If I just take it one day at a time, building exercise into my routine feels doable.

- I'm too busy/I have no time → My time is precious, and that's why I make time to be healthy.

- It's not working/It's going to take a long time until I see results → I know if I'm consistent, I will make progress over time.

- I'm not athletic/not built for it → Movement looks different from person to person, and I'm going to find an exercise that works for my body.

Try lots of different things that get your heart pumping. Here are some of the most popular exercises:

Team Activities	Solo Activities	Great With a Buddy!
Basketball	Dancing	Pilates
Football	Tai Chi	Yoga
Soccer	Jogging	Barre
Martial Arts	Skateboarding	Roller-skating
Volleyball	Swimming	Nature Walks
Hockey	Weight-lifting	Hiking
Pickleball	Figure-skating	Tennis
Baseball	Gardening	Biking
Kickball	Exercise Videos	Kayaking
Basketball	Power walking	Table tennis

Movement Hack: Give Yourself Daily Challenges.

Squeeze in bonus opportunities for movement throughout the day, by setting small challenges for yourself.

Examples of Daily Challenges:

- I'm going to take the stairs to class instead of the elevator.

- This week, I'll walk to the store instead of driving.

- I'm going to try biking to school.

- During each commercial break tonight, I'll do 20 jumping jacks.

- I'll take the dog for a quick walk before I head to school.

- When my alarm goes off, I'll do 10 push-ups before I start getting ready for the day.

Acts of Kindness: Paying It Forward

Not all of the Significant Six habits cause you to break into a sweat, like the exercise habit. You can practice this fourth idea without lifting a finger.

You know that warm fuzzy feeling you get when you do things like helping out someone in need, volunteering your time, and donating a few dollars to good causes?

That's your brain bursting with happiness hormones.

Did you know that spreading a little kindness can serve as an all-natural pick-me-up? Scientists have uncovered a fascinating connection between engaging in helping others and improved well being—the nicer we are to the people and environment around us, the happier we become!

Studies suggest that when you treat others with care and consideration your brain releases "feel good" chemicals like dopamine and oxytocin to reduce stress. Kindness isn't just great for those around us either—performing random acts of selflessness increases our own sense of worthiness too!

So why not get your kind on?

Ideas to Spread Kindness:

Spreading kindness is simple and doesn't need to take a lot of time or effort (and it doesn't even have to be face-to-face!). Here are some ideas to get you started:

- Send a thank you card or note to someone who has made an impact on your life.

- Offer to help a family member with their errands or chores.

- Start a compliment chain by telling someone something nice and asking them to do the same for another person.

- Donate your time or money to a cause close to your heart.

- Buy a friend's coffee or lunch.

- Hold the door for someone.

- Clean out your closet and find things you've outgrown to donate to a good cause.

- Compliment someone on their outfit or hairstyle.

- Offer to walk your neighbor's pet when they're out of town.

- Send a card to a grandparent.

- Give a warm meal to someone in need.

- Leave a five-star review online.

- Pick up litter on the street.

Journaling: A Mighty Outlet

Forget what you think you know about journaling., which is fifth on our list of The Significant Six.

No, this isn't your English class journal where you have to worry about things like handwriting and spelling. Your journal can be neat or sloppy, it can include words, symbols, and pictures, or it can jump from thoughts and worries to dreams and aspirations.

Your journal is purely for your brain. Journaling for yourself means giving yourself time to slow down and think about your thoughts one at a time. It's a place where you can sort out all the "stuff" that clouds up your mind throughout the day.

The beauty of journaling is that it's completely up to you—you can make your journal as formal or informal as you please. You can include entries about things like what happened during the day, how social situations made you feel, and any thoughts or feelings associated with them.

Research has shown time and again that journaling brings countless benefits to mental health.

A study published in the *Journal of Personality and Social* Psychology suggests that people who journal for 15 minutes at least three times a week have reported positive effects on social anxiety, depression, and overall life-satisfaction. So why wouldn't you want to curl up with a journal and do some reflecting once in a while?

And once you get past the awkward fact that you're not actually talking to anyone but yourself, you might find that journaling feels like a safe place. Writing down your feelings allows them to come to the surface without any pressure.

You can also experience sweet benefits like:

- Increased overall well-being.
- Working through complex emotions.
- Identifying patterns of thinking.
- Getting to know yourself.
- Let out thoughts and emotions to create more space in your mind.

Making It Into a Ritual

Let's be honest—if you don't do it often, journaling can feel... *weird*. You're essentially having a conversation with *yourself*. It's one of those things in life where you just have to roll with it. Embrace it. Work through the strangeness of it. After that, the rest is easy.

Step 1: Get a notebook and pen, or open up a blank document on your phone or computer.

Step 2: Choose a journaling method and start writing.

Step 3: Re-read at any point without judgment to reflect on your thoughts and experiences.

How Do I Get Started with Journaling?

Obviously, the hardest step is the writing part, so here are some ideas to get you started:

- **Gratitude Journaling:** It's easy to get hung up on negative thinking, but gratitude journaling helps you take control of unhelpful negative thoughts.

You can create an open "Gratitude List": Start a list with all the things you're grateful for in your life and why and keep adding to them over the days as you discover more things worth being grateful for. Or, think of three things you are grateful for each day, and why, and log into your journal.

- **Free Writing:** If you're feeling blocked, free writing can help give your thoughts and feelings an outlet. Set a timer and write without stopping for a few minutes and see what ideas come out.
- **Scripting:** This one is fun because you get to interact with future-you. Write out a scene from the perspective of future-you, building a world where you've accomplished your goals and you're living your ideal life.

Here are some possible prompts: What is your future self like? What are your best future characteristics? What did your future self achieve? How many friends does she/he have? What do people love about him/her? What does future-you do for a living? Use as many sensory details as you can to bring the vision to life on the page.

- **Anxious Thought Journaling:** If there's an event coming up that's making you anxious, write your feelings about it before it happens.

For instance, say you're nervous about going to a party. Here are some steps to start with Anxious Thought Journaling:

Step 1: Start writing what you're nervous about—*Someone I don't know might talk to me—eek!*

Step 2: Write some opposing thoughts—*Who knows—I might make a friend and it might not be so bad.*

Step 3: Write steps you can take to make the experience easier—*I'll make sure I get a good night's sleep and exercise before going to the party to stay energized. To avoid feeling unnecessary* *stress, I'll avoid drinks high in caffeine and I'll prepare conversation starters. If things go south and I start feeling anxious, I'll go to the bathroom to freshen up and take a break.*

Step 4: After the event is over, write how it went. How did you feel? Did you make any mistakes? Write how you think you should react next time you're in the situation. This helps you realize an important truth about your brain: the thing you say to yourself in your head are exaggerated compared with reality!

Journaling should be something you feel non-judgement about, like dancing in your room with the doors closed, or singing in the shower when no one's home. Just do it and forget about everyone else in the world and what they think.

Pro Journaling Tips to Get You Started

- **Find a comfortable writing spot.** Wherever you feel most relaxed and free to express yourself.
- **Pick a prompt.** Choose something random or pick a prompt that fits your emotions in the moment. You can also fly by the seat of your pants and just start writing—there are no rules.
- **Set a timer.** Start with 10-15 minutes of journaling and adjust it as you become more comfortable with the process.
- **Write like no one is reading (because they're not!)** Don't worry about saying things perfectly or agonize over handwriting—that's not what this journal is about. You don't even have to use words all the time–doodle, sketch, or do whatever feels right.
- **Resist the need to edit.** You don't need to make things clearer or grammatically correct. Remember, this is for your brain only.
- **Make it a habit by keeping at it.** Make journaling a part of your routine to reap the most benefits. With practice, it'll come easier and you'll start looking forward to this time with yourself.

Mindfulness: What Is It, Really?

Mindfulness is the last of the Significant Six habits to help with anxiety, and you can consider it a superpower: Declutter your mind with mindfulness meditation.

Can you imagine if you had never cleaned your bedroom since you were born? There would be so much random, unnecessary junk cluttering up your space! Believe it or not, cleaning out your brain is just as important as cleaning out your room.

That's where mindfulness comes in.

Mindfulness means being thoughtful and attentive to the present moment. When you don't stress about the past or the future, it's sort of like "rinsing" your brain of all the extra stuff it doesn't need at that time. From brushing your teeth to walking the dog, mindfulness is a way of life that can enrich virtually anything you do.

When you become aware of your present thoughts and feelings in a non-judgmental way, it's like a karate chop that cuts off your brain from ruminating and worrying. The best part? *You don't have to become a master-guru meditator hovering above the ground in lotus position to benefit from it.* Wherever you are starting right now is the perfect place, so just take it one step at a time!

Meditation is More Powerful Than You Think

With so many benefits that affect nearly every aspect of your life, you'll wonder why you didn't start practicing mindfulness meditation sooner. You'll find it:

- Reduces cortisol while boosting serotonin, alleviating stress and anxiety.
- Lowers blood pressure and increases heart health.
- Improves sleep quality and helps you sleep longer.
- Helps your attention and concentration throughout the day.
- Allows you to step back, so you can learn to notice thoughts and feelings and without being over-taken by them.

Exercise: 5-Minute Sensory Meditation

Step 1: Find somewhere quiet where you can sit in peace.

Step 2: Take a comfortable seat or lie down.

Step 3: Close your eyes and breathe deeply a few times. Then, let your breath come back to its normal pattern.

Step 4: Let any thoughts that come up pass through without judgment. When your mind wanders (which it will, and that's okay), refocus your attention on your breath. Stay in that moment for a few minutes, just focusing on and observing your breath.

Step 5: Open your eyes and bring your attention to your senses. Start by naming (in your head) what you can see. Then, move through your other senses.

What does the air feel like? What does it smell like? Are there cars driving by? Can you hear birds chirping? Is there any taste in your mouth? Take note of everything, but don't feel as though you have to do anything. Just *notice it*.

Step 6: Now turn your attention inward. Can you feel your heart beating? How does your breathing sound and feel? Do you notice your body moving with each breath? How does your body feel? Can you feel your body weight against the ground or surface beneath you? Stay there in that moment, feel the ground support you, for as long as you can.

Step 7: That's it—you did mindfulness meditation by just taking notice of your body and the world around you. You trained your brain to be more present simply by *existing* and clearing your mind of unnecessary information.

Step 8: Give yourself a fist bump.

Is Mindful Eating a Thing?
Yes, you bet it is!

When's the last time you zoned out while eating snacks in front of the television? No shame—it happens to people all the time. But it's not helping your physical or mental health, and that's where mindful eating can be a game-changer.

Mindful eating uses some of the same skills you used in the mindfulness meditation exercise: noticing body-related sensations, focusing on being in the moment, and noting your thoughts and feelings about food while you eat.

And it's excellent for you, too! Mindful eating can:

- Improve digestion.
- Keep you full for longer, indirectly aiding in maintaining healthy weight.
- Influence you to make wiser choices about what and when you eat.
- Help build a healthier relationship with food.

Exercise: Let's Practice Mindful Eating

Paying attention to your food while you eat it isn't quite as simple as it sounds. From preparation to serving and enjoying, there are distractions just waiting to snag your attention, causing you to miss out on important cues from your body that may signal everything from pleasure to fullness.

We won't leave you hanging to figure it out on your own, though! So here's an exercise that can help you build your mindful eating muscles.

Step 1: Grab some berries from the fridge. Pluck one berry from the bunch and set it down in front of you.

Step 2: WAIT! Do not throw a handful of berries into your mouth. (Tough when they're just looking at you like they can't wait to be eaten, but trust us—there's a good reason to hold off).

Step 3: Imagine you're an alien and you've never seen a berry before—time to tap into your brain's powerful curiosity signals.

Step 4: Take a moment to tap into your breath and relax your body.

Step 5: Time to engage with the berry—pick it up. Feel its weight in your hand.

Step 6: Examine the berry from the perspective of an alien. What colors, textures, and smells do you observe? Are there dimples, ridges, smooth parts, or dull parts?

Step 7: Roll the berry between your fingers and lift it to your ear—what sound does it make?

Step 8: Now that you've played with it for a few seconds, is it making your fingers sticky? Are there juices rolling down your hand? Is the berry hot, cold, or room temperature? How does it feel against your skin?

Step 9: At long last—your alien-self is ready to taste test this strange fruit. Place the berry in your mouth, but don't bite down. Hold it on your tongue for a few moments and let it roll around your mouth. What does it taste like? Is your mouth salivating? Is your brain saying, "Bite down already?!"

Step 10: Fine, you can FINALLY bite down, just once. What do you notice? What burst of new flavors and sensations do you experience? Chew slowly and notice what each bite brings until it's liquified and then swallow.

Step 11: Reflect on the berry. If you were an alien eating a berry for the first time, would you want to eat one again? As a human, what kinds of emotions and sensations did you experience while you ate?

Well done! You've just practiced mindful eating!

A Mindful Walk

Have you ever stopped to consider what a miraculous thing it is to walk? Hundreds of muscles work together to propel you forward, feet lifting and falling, lifting and falling, over and over. The world around you changes with each step, sometimes affecting your breath or emotions.

A gentle breeze on your skin, the sound of children laughing, the smell of someone barbequing in the backyard—all these sensations make mindful walking a delightful way to de-stress and re-center.

But most people let their minds start to stray after the first few minutes. Some people even take out their phones to scroll and walk at the same time, completely missing out on tons of fabulous benefits like:

- Reduced blood pressure and heart rate.
- Feelings of happiness thanks to serotonin.
- Improved mood and lowered feelings of stress.
- Better quality sleep.

Exercise: Let's Go on a Mindful Walk

If you want the full benefits of mindful walking, start by putting your phone away—you won't need it for this!

Step 1: choose outside if possible, so you can get the full benefits of sunlight and fresh air.

Step 2: Start by walking a little bit slower than usual.

Step 3: Focus on your breathing as you walk and pay attention to the sensations of each step. What does your foot feel like inside your shoe? What does the pavement or ground feel like beneath your feet? Is it smooth or gravel? Is it wet or dry?

Do you feel the clothes rubbing against your skin as you walk? How does it feel? How does the temperature feel on your skin? Do you feel the breeze moving through your hair?

Step 4: What do you see happening around you? What sounds do you hear? What smells do you notice? What does it feel like to be you in this exact moment, walking around in the world? Simply take a mental notes of these things.

Step 5: If thoughts about things that happened during your day pop into your mind, acknowledge them and bring your attention back to the present moment.

Step 6: Walk yourself safely back home and notice how you feel. Did you see or experience anything interesting that you wouldn't have normally noticed? Is it something you would like to do again?

The End of Chapter 5
And you've made it through another chapter!

You might be thinking, oof that was a lot, I don't know if I can do it all. Don't worry, it doesn't have to be an all-or-nothing approach—every small change counts. Maybe you start by picking one or two things you'd like to work on first, then gradually add as you feel ready. Making small improvements one at a time can add up to big benefits in the long run.

See you in the final chapter!

CHAPTER 6

Your Quest For Support

Isa's Request

Isa was dead-tired when she got home from the dance. She came through the door as quietly as she could in her bare feet, shoes dangling by the straps in one hand.

She had done her best to hide in the corner of the gym as far away from the dance floor as she could manage, but her friends insisted "The Three Amigas" stick together.

"Isa, come dance with us," Chloe yelled over the bumping music after Isa first tried to disappear.

"Yeah, you only get to go to your 9th-grade homecoming dance once in a lifetime," Marcy added.

"Eh, I'll look silly. I don't know how to dance," Isa admitted, feeling ashamed.

The other two girls giggled.

"You're supposed to look silly, see?" Chloe pointed to the dance floor, where Isa observed a number of questionable dance moves.

"I call that one the "Lean and Bounce." Marcy pointed to a circle of girls shifting their weight from side to side along with every down beat of the music, occasionally snapping their fingers or bobbing their heads.

"That one's the Shivering Shimmy!" Chloe blurted out before bursting into a fit of laughter. She motioned towards a boy with his arms open wide, shaking his hips madly from left to right as he sang along, his loose pink tie wagging along wildly with each move.

"That one's a doozy," Marcy said, dabbing tears of laughter from her eyes. She motioned to another boy with his arms locked straight up above his head, flicking his wrists back and forth as he did a kind of duck walk across the dance floor.

"What should we call that one?" Chloe asked, turning to Isa.

Isa, who, by that point, was laughing harder than she'd ever laughed in her life, managed to choke out the words, "The D-Dorky Duck?"

A moment of silence hung in the air before all three girls erupted in hysterical giggles.

After catching her breath, Marcy hooked one arm through Isa's elbow and the other through Chloe's and said, "Come on, amigas—to the dance floor!"

Isa closed her eyes and made the leap. She danced awkwardly with her friends at first, feeling self-conscious. But after a while, she couldn't help but loosen up a bit. Everyone around her seemed to embrace the silliness of it all, and eventually, she danced like she'd never danced before.

"Isa, how was homecoming?"

Lost in her memories of the evening, Isa returned to earth and closed the door. She turned to see her mother, looking hopeful but tentative.

"It was…" Isa thought for a moment.

"The best night of my life."

Her mother raised an eyebrow and smiled ear to ear.

"Really?"

"I wish—I wish I had more memories like that."

Isa's joy suddenly turned to sadness. She knew it was just a fluke—she'd just been pretending to be a "normal" girl for one night, but now it was time to go back to the "real" her.

"Well of course, sweetheart. You'll make lots of fun memories in high school."

"I'm not so sure that I will," Isa muttered.

"Why would you say such a thing?"

Isa's voice was suddenly shaky, her hands were sweaty, and she stared straight at her feet. She wasn't sure her mom would understand, or even believe her, but she decided to go for it.

"Something's wrong with me, mom. But I'm not sure what."

Her mother looked at her for a long moment and said, "There's nothing wrong with you, honey. Tell me what you mean?"

"Well, before I went to the dance, I thought I was going to have a heart attack. I had fun while I was there, but now that I'm home, I know I'll just go back to being the same shy, scared person I always am around people."

Taking Isa by surprise, her mom gave her a big hug. Isa felt tears swelling in her eyes.

"Mom, I want to be more *confident*," Isa stated firmly.

"I don't want to hide anymore. I want to make the most of my time in high school, but I just don't know how to change."

Her mother wiped the tears from Isa's eyes.

"I'm proud of you for telling me what you're feeling, Isa. Let's make a plan."

Isa wasn't sure what kind of plan her mother had in mind, but sharing how she really felt seemed to lift the weight of the world off her shoulders. She didn't know it yet, but that one moment of honesty with her mother was about to change the rest of Isa's life.

Jeremy's Realization

When Ashton's mom dropped him back off at home after the dance, Jeremy let out a huge sigh of relief. He stood at the doorway of his house for what seemed like forever, long after his friends had driven off.

All night, he'd been trying to figure out what to say to Shania, and his brain now felt like it was running on empty.

When they entered the gym, Jeremy's instinct was to turn right back around. The music boomed, hundreds of kids mingled and danced, and the air was thick with sweat and laughter—it was his nightmare.

But Shania took his hand and led the group to a row of metal folding chairs against the wall. After setting down their purses and jackets, Jeremy and Shania watched their friends get up one-by-one and head to the dance floor with their dates.

Shania touched his arm and nudged him toward the dance floor, but Jeremy couldn't budge. He desperately wanted to dance with Shania and the rest of the group, but felt completely paralyzed.

"It's not so bad once you're out there," Shania said, trying to look Jeremy in the eye. Jeremy noticed, but couldn't bring himself to return the gaze.

All he could think about was what she'd think of him once he was out on the dance floor. A million self-defeating thoughts raced across his mind as though an evil hamster wheel of doubt spun endlessly in his brain.

What if his dance moves were terrible? What if he got too sweaty? Too nervous? Didn't she already think he was weird?

Shania sighed and asked if he wanted any punch. He knew what he wanted to say, but the right words didn't come out.

"I'm f-f-fine, tha-thanks," Jeremy stammered.

Shania said, "Okay," and smiled politely before heading off. A few minutes later, Jeremy saw her dancing with the group, no punch glass in hand.

She clearly just wanted to get away from him, right?

Afraid she'd see him looking at her, he opted to stare at his shoes for a while.

"Jer, my man, you're missing out on the fun!"

Ashton headed toward him, hair wildly tussled about his head, pink tie dangling precariously from his neck.

"Come on, I promise my moves will make everyone laugh *way* harder than yours will."

Ashton put his hands on his hips and did a little swivel, and Jeremy couldn't help but crack a smile.

"I remember in elementary school, Mrs. Gladwell's 3rd grade end-of-year party," Ashton said nostalgically, "you had some killer dance moves!"

Jeremy remembered that day fondly, too. But that was before he knew he was doomed to a lifetime of awkwardness—before he realized how weird and stupid he could be.

"Just close your eyes and pretend!"

Against his will, Jeremy nodded and stood up to follow Ashton back to the dance floor.

No, the voices in his head started screaming, *you're walking straight into a trap!*

To his horror, several members of their group clapped when they saw him. Shania's face lit up, and before he could run back to the metal chairs, she'd already grabbed his hand.

Without speaking, she started swaying his hand back and forth to the cadence of the music. He stood frozen at first, unsure what the rest of his body was supposed to do.

*Wait...*the voice in his head started, *you're still alive? This isn't so bad...I guess.*

With that, he started tapping his foot and bobbing his head.

Hey, I kind of like this song, the voice added.

Before he knew it, he was dancing—full blown, every-limb-doing-its-part-to-move-to-the-music- dancing. At times, he had no idea what his body was doing, and knew that he looked ridiculous.

But if he was honest, everyone around him did too.

When the DJ played one of Shania's favorite songs, she began hopping up and down like a kid on a pogo stick and doing the wave with her arms. Ashton was all hips, and kept clearing out spots around him as people dodged his experimental disco moves.

A few girls stood off the side watching and laughing, but for once in his life, it didn't make Jeremy want to run and hide. Soon, they joined in on the dance floor, too.

Jeremy couldn't believe he'd actually managed to dance with everyone. As he stood in the doorway of his house, his mind raced.

He'd even given Shania his phone number at the end of the night in case she wanted to hang out again.

As he caught his breath, his father opened the door.

"Is that you out here, Jer? How was it, buddy?"

Jeremy stared for a moment before a smile crept across his lips.

"It was fun."

"Well get in here and tell me all about it!"

Jeremy followed his father to the living room and collapsed to the couch. All that dancing and socializing had really worn him out. After retelling the highlights of his evening, Jeremy at last revealed, "I gave a girl my phone number."

But when he said it, the words fell flat. He wasn't excited about it—in fact, he was downright terrified. He already felt defeated.

Sure, he'd managed to socialize at the dance. But carrying on a one-on-one conversation alone with a girl he liked was a *completely different thing*. Ashton couldn't be there to bring him out of his shell every single time.

Jeremy felt ready to *do something about it.*

But what would his parents say? He was worried his father might tell him to buck up and get over it.

"Dad, I've been kind of struggling with something for a little while. It's hard to explain," Jeremy thought about saying.

"Uh huh, sure. Why are you always trying to pull one over on us? Sounds like you're just trying to wriggle your way out of going to school again" he imagined his dad saying back to him.

Or even, "Dad, sometimes if there's an event coming up where there's going to be lots of people I don't know, my stomach balls up into knots, and I lie awake in bed all night panicking about how dumb I'll look if I say the wrong thing."

"Oh perfect," his imaginary father said with a scoff, "now my son doesn't know how to socialize like a normal person on top of all his other shenanigans. How could I have failed so miserably as a father?"

And please, Jeremy thought, *don't let it go like this:* "Hey, I'm drowning over here. Going to school, attending parties, it's all overwhelming and I need help. The way my body and brain react are holding me back, and I'd like to learn how to manage these feelings."

"Bah, when I was a teenager, I felt a little shy around other people, too. It's nothing, don't worry about it, toughen up and move on. You'll outgrow it."

His brain tried the scenario one more time.

"I'd like to share something I'm dealing with right now because I'm interested in learning how to overcome it and I'm hoping you can help."

"What's going on, Jer Bear? You know I'm happy to help you out."

That version didn't seem so bad, but what were the chances his dad would be supportive? How could he word it perfectly so that his dad didn't think he was lying, didn't feel as though he'd failed as a parent, and didn't belittle what he was going through?

I just have to go for it, Jeremy thought. *Maybe it won't be perfect, but I'm going to try and explain what's going on the best I can.*

How Do I Talk to Others About What's Going on With Me?

One of the scariest parts about dealing with SAD is figuring out how to talk to your people about what's going on. Let's be honest—sometimes, it feels downright *embarrassing* to share your feelings with other people.

Jeremy struggled with this exact dilemma—*What if I don't word things perfectly? What if it makes me sound weird? Will they get mad at me like I've done something wrong? What if they don't believe me?*

Don't worry—opening up is the first step to feeling better.

The adults in your life want the best for you. And reaching out for help managing your SAD symptoms is the absolute *best* thing you can do for yourself right now. You may feel most comfortable talking to your parents, a guidance counselor, or even a family friend.

No matter who you talk to, the most important part is that you *start talking about it*. If you've tried self-help (like the strategies you've learned in this book) but nothing seems to be working, the next step is being honest about what you need with the people who care about you most.

By expressing your needs to your loved ones, you can begin the path to therapy (more on that in a bit).

What's Stopping You from Talking to Your Parents About SAD?

Can you relate to the fears that Jeremy had about talking with his parents about what's going on?

First, Jeremy was worried his dad would accuse him of lying. Then he imagined he'd make his dad feel as though he had failed as a parent. But his biggest fear of all was that his old man would basically just say "toughen up, buttercup" and expect him to magically snap out of it.

But Jeremy knows that SAD symptoms and typical teen shyness aren't the same thing.

Challenge: What's Holding You Back?

Think about the things holding you back from talking openly with the adults you trust most. Put a check next to some of the reasons stopping you from talking to others about your SAD symptoms.

- ___ Afraid of how they will react.

- ___ Worried that they won't believe you.

- ___ Expecting they will be disappointed.

- ___ Not wanting to stress them out.

- ___ Fear that they will judge you.

- ___ Worried they will ask a ton of questions.

- ___ Afraid they will blame themselves.

- ___ Anxious they will invalidate your feelings or dismiss them.

- ___ Concerned you will appear weak and vulnerable.

- _____.

(fill in your own)

Quick tips:

- You can write down a list of reasons why you feel you need help and give it to a person you trust.
- You can write a letter to your parents explaining that you are worried they might not take your problems seriously.
- You can talk to your parents about why you think you're struggling and why you need some extra support.
- If your parents really don't understand, talk to another adult, like a guidance counselor or teacher.

Challenging your concerns

"Won't They Be Let Down or Disappointed?"

It may be hard for your parents to hear that their child is struggling—no one wants to see someone they love suffering. **But this doesn't mean they're mad or upset with you**.

Quick tips:

- If you tell them your fears about making them upset, it may help them respond better.

  Your parents might not know how to react or what it means to get help for mental health. Just keep speaking up! They love you and will start to understand over time.

"They Have Enough to Worry About"

Yes, your parents do have adult responsibilities, and they may seem stressed sometimes. **But they want you to succeed, no matter what.** Your wellbeing is important and deserves attention—no matter what else is going on at home.

Quick tips:

- If you're worried about stressing out your parents, pick a time to talk when things are calm.
- Come prepared to share information about what you're going through and what kind of help you would like.

"What if They Ask a Lot of Questions?"
Even if they do ask a lot of questions, **you don't have to answer all of them.** There are a lot of reasons why you may not want to tell your parents *every single detail* about what's going on!

Quick tips:

- You can tell your parents that you really don't know how to talk about your feelings, but a therapist or counselor can help you to answer their questions.
- Create a plan for how to talk to them and write down how you're feeling so you don't feel so "on-the-spot."

How To Talk About SAD

This might shock you, but **you're not the only one struggling to find the words.** *Most* teenagers find it challenging to talk about how they feel. But don't panic—we've got you covered. By the time you finish this section, you'll have all the tools you need to discuss your feelings to an adult you trust.

Step 1: Pick the right time and place. Choose a time and place that you know will allow the other person to fully listen to what you have to say. Be sure there aren't too many distractions. For instance, you could bring up the conversation after dinner as you're helping your parents clean up the kitchen. Or, you could bring it up one-on-one while you're driving home in the car, where you could continue the conversation if needed.

Step 2: Remember your coping strategies. Breathe. Pause and take a deep, filling breath. If you can feel your nervous system ramping up for fight, flight, or freeze (your heart is racing, your breathing is fast, your palms are sweaty, etc.), then use your coping skills from the previous chapters to soothe your nervous system before heading into the conversation.

Step 3: Describe what you're going through and be as clear as possible. Use real examples of your experiences to help your parents understand your needs. Be specific. For instance, "When I go to school and someone talks to me that I don't know, my stomach feels upset, my breathing gets fast, and I start having stressful thoughts. That makes it difficult to talk to people. I wish I didn't feel like this."

Be clear and direct about your situation, making it easier for your parents to understand without guessing. It's helpful to write down examples in advance.

Step 4: Clearly express, "I need help." Don't stress about figuring out *why* you're feeling like this—that's not important at this point. Instead, be honest and say, "I want to see someone who can help. I want to learn some tips from a professional so I can start feeling better."

If they tell you what you're feeling is normal—everyone gets nervous or sad sometimes— remind them that you know it's more serious than that. Your feelings are holding you back from being happy and doing the things you want to do.

Step 5: Remember that you can take a break if you need to. If they don't get the whole picture during your first conversation, *that's okay*. Keep talking about it and being open. Sometimes it's tough to get your parents to listen, right?

If you tried talking to your parents about something that's been bugging you, but it didn't go as planned, don't give up just yet. You can *totally* try again. But this time, set up a specific time to chat so your parents can give you their full attention.

If that still doesn't work, don't sweat it. You can reach out to another trusted adult like a cool aunt or uncle, your favorite teacher, or even the school psychologist. They can help you express how you're feeling and find ways to get your parents to understand.

Just remember, even if you're struggling at school or with something else, there are always people who care and want to help you succeed. Don't be afraid to speak up and get the support you deserve even if you have to do it more than once.

Seeking Therapy

Some teens believe social anxiety disorder will just vanish into thin air, like a magic trick performed by the Great Houdini. If you think your excessive shyness and anxiety in social situations is just a temporary phase that will magically disappear (but then it doesn't), then it's time to get real.

Pretty much everyone can benefit from some form of therapy—especially teens wrangling the symptoms of SAD.

Maybe you're thinking, *it's better to keep my social anxiety tucked away in secret than to lay all my cards on the table.* You may even downplay your symptoms, thinking they're just a pesky annoyance that will fade away like a bad fashion trend.

While you do score a point for wishful thinking, you need to keep in mind that SAD is a legit mental health condition that deserves attention and proper care.

It's time to wave the magic wand of awareness, seek help from the pros, and manage your social anxiety symptoms for good.

Challenge: What Are Your Biggest Fears About Going to Therapy?

- ___ Afraid that your therapist will judge you.

- ___ Stigma associated with going to therapy.

- ___ Afraid of what your friends will think about you if they know you're in therapy.

- ___ Feeling as though your therapist won't understand or will invalidate you.

- ___ Worried that therapy will make you feel worse.

- ___ Fear of trusting someone new.

- ___ Don't like the idea of opening up to someone you don't know.

- ___ Don't think therapy will help.

- ___ Fear of facing your problems.

- ___ It all sounds so overwhelming.

How Do You Know if it's Time to Seek Therapy?

If you're feeling as though you're constantly starring in a one-person show called "Overwhelmed and Anxious," tossing and turning like a pro wrestler at night when you're trying to sleep, having nightmares and visions about social situations that would give Stephen King a run for his money, and your stomach is staging a never-ending protest, then it *might* just be time to consider therapy.

Okay fine—*it's definitely time to consider therapy.*

It's like a mental health alarm clock telling you, "Hey, it's time to hit the pause button and get some professional support!" Because here's the thing: you deserve to be the star of a feel-good show called "Thriving and Fabulous!"

If you find yourself regularly experiencing symptoms of panic attacks, such as a rapid or pounding heartbeat, difficulty breathing, profuse sweating, trembling or shaking, and that gut feeling that something bad is about to happen and you can't shake it off, *it's time to consider seeking therapy.*

Finally, if self-help tools aren't cutting it, anxiety is dragging you down, relationships are a puzzle, emotions are all over the place, work/school is suffering, or unhealthy coping mechanisms are creeping in, *therapy can be the biggest help ever.*

You don't have to face it all alone—therapy offers support, tools, and strategies to navigate life's challenges. Whether it's thoughts of giving up on yourself or dreading things you used to enjoy, therapy can make a difference.

You can take charge of your mental health and well-being so you can build the life you dream of having without SAD standing in your way.

Challenge: List Some Reasons You Think You Might Be Ready for therapy.

_____

_____

_____

_____

_____

_____

_____

_____

Therapy is Not as Bad as You Think

Here's some good news: even some of your favorite celebrities go to therapy! Yep, it's true. Movie stars, singers, athletes, you name it, they've been there.

So if you're feeling a little apprehensive or nervous about seeking help, just know that you're not alone. It's totally normal to feel that way.

But therapy is a proactive and empowering step towards taking care of yourself. It's like hitting the reset button on your mind and emotions and giving yourself the tools you need to thrive.

And when you go to therapy, you won't be judged or criticized. Therapists are trained to provide a safe and supportive space for you to express yourself. They're like your own personal cheerleaders, helping you build resilience and overcome challenges.

You deserve to feel happy and healthy, and there's absolutely no shame in seeking help. In fact, it's one of the bravest and strongest things you can do for yourself.

Challenging Your Concerns

"What if My Therapist Invalidates Me?"
We totally get it—opening up about your social anxiety to a therapist can make you feel super scared and vulnerable, like jumping into the deep end of a pool without knowing how to swim.

But here's the thing: Therapists are like expert swimmers or lifeguards. They've seen it all before, and they're there to help you learn how to float, doggy paddle, and swim laps like a pro. They won't judge you or throw you in the deep end without a life vest.

They'll be there for you, every step of the way, to help you build your confidence, manage your anxiety, and feel comfortable in your own skin.

"I Don't Want to Open Up to a Total Stranger"
Spill your guts to a total stranger? We know what you're thinking—who the heck in their right mind wants to do that! Talking to a therapist can feel a little bit like going on a blind date—it's exciting, nerve-wracking,

and kinda weird all at once. But trust us, therapy is like a magic mirror that can help you see yourself more clearly and understand your thoughts and feelings in a whole new way.

It's totally normal to feel a little anxious or awkward about opening up to a therapist. It's like taking off your armor and revealing your vulnerabilities to a stranger. However, good therapists won't attack while your shield is down. They're expert listeners who will give you all the time and space you need to share your thoughts and feelings at your own pace.

So embrace the weirdness of it all.

"What if Confronting My Anxiety Makes it Worse?"

Think about working out. When you start exercising, your muscles might ache and feel sore. But that's because you're using muscles that you haven't used before or haven't used in a long time. And over time, as you continue to work out, your muscles get stronger, and the discomfort goes away.

It's the same way with therapy. When you start confronting your anxiety, it might feel uncomfortable at first. But as you continue to work through it with your therapist, you'll start to feel stronger and more in control of your thoughts and feelings. Remember, it's okay to feel uncomfortable because it means you're making progress towards feeling better.

"Going to Therapy Means I'm Weak"

When it comes to learning things like trigonometry, foreign languages, or essay writing, things can get a little hairy.

You're not born knowing sine, cosine, and tangent. If French isn't your first language, then you can't just read a book about French and expect to be a fluent speaker. And literary essays? Forget about it—no one's ever written one without a teacher showing them the ropes first.

Would you tell someone they're weak for needing a tutor or teacher to show them how to do these things? No way!

Seeking help is a sign of strength, not weakness. Only a small percentage of people with social anxiety disorder get help quickly, and many suffer for years before seeking treatment. That would be like never going to a single trigonometry class and then expecting yourself to pass the test at the end of the year—what a nightmare!

Choosing therapy means taking things into your own hands. You're making the decision to change your life, and not many people are brave enough to do that. So in reality, going to therapy is a sign of brute strength.

Plus, the idea that you should handle life's challenges all on your own is outdated.

"Will Therapy Even Help?"

Of course you're wondering whether therapy will help—if you've never done it before, then it's natural to have your doubts. *Will I be wasting my time? What if I'm a lost cause that no one can help? What if I'm the one hopeless case in the whole history of therapy?*

Remember this: Therapists are trained professionals who understand anxiety and know exactly how to support you through tough thoughts and feelings. Think about the last time you went to the doctor. When the doctor gives a shot or prescribes medication, most of us don't bat an eyelash about it.

Do the patients fully understand the biological and chemical processes involved in making these treatments work? Heck no—that takes *years* of studying and then more years of practice. That's why these doctors went to medical school in the first place.

And by the way, your therapist has to go through *years* of schooling and practice, too. They've studied, trained, and dedicated their lives to understanding the complexities of the human mind. So let these pros do their job and just trust the process.

"If I Get Diagnosed With SAD, Will I Have It Forever?"

Ever had a bad haircut before? We're talking bangs that don't want to stay in place, hair sticking up in places where it should lay flat, the whole nine years. We've all been there.

But do haircuts last forever? Thankfully, they sure don't!

Just because you get diagnosed with social anxiety disorder (SAD) doesn't mean you're stuck with it for life. As time passes and you allow therapy to do its job, then you'll notice yourself starting to feel better.

And guess what? The stats are on your side. According to the National Alliance on Mental Illness, 70% to 90% of people who seek treatment for mental health problems recover. So don't let the fear of a diagnosis hold you back from getting the help you need to thrive as your best self.

"What if My Therapist Wants Me to Make Changes When I'm Not Ready?"

A lot of people think that therapy requires them to immediately stop self-sabotaging behaviors, like avoiding social situations or using earphones in public to avoid talking to others.

Relax! therapists understand that change takes time and *will meet you where you're at*. They'll work with you when you're ready and willing to change.

For example, if you're not comfortable meeting in person, they might offer virtual sessions until you feel ready. Your therapist will help you make small changes at your own pace and will tailor the process to your needs. If something doesn't feel right, you can speak up, and they'll adjust their approach to accommodate you.

"What if I Don't Click With My Therapist?"
Do you always buy the first pair of shoes you try on at the store? No way—some might be the wrong size, some might be uncomfortable. Finding the right therapist is a bit like trying on shoes —you might need to test out a few before you find the perfect fit. It's so important to feel comfortable talking with your therapist, otherwise you won't be able to open up about the things that matter most.

Many therapists offer free mini-consultations to get a feel for their style and approach. Don't be shy—ask them any questions you have! It's cool to "shop around" for a therapist, as they know it's essential to find someone you vibe with. Trust your instincts and choose the one who makes you feel safe and understood.

"What if I Feel Worse After Therapy?"
Starting therapy might feel scary, like cleaning out a super messy closet. At first, it could seem overwhelming, and you might wonder if it's even worth it.

Here's the deal: Therapy can be like learning to drive—things might get a bit rocky before they smooth out. Just like organizing that chaotic closet, you'll start to let go of what's not needed and rework the rest until you're feeling better and functioning well.

It's totally normal to feel some resistance or get defensive during therapy—those feelings are there to protect you. Just remember to be open with your therapist, stick with it, and trust that growth and relief are coming your way.

"Once I Start Therapy, Will I Have to Go Forever?"
Therapy isn't a forever thing, so don't stress about spending years in sessions. Therapists want to see you make progress and live your best life, too! In fact, the main goal of therapy is to eventually say "goodbye."

The time you spend with a therapist depends on the issues you're working on, your commitment, and the type of therapy. Some peeps might stick around for self-exploration or to work on other areas of their life, but that's totally up to you. Just remember, therapy is all about helping you grow and move forward.

"What Will My Friends Think if They Find out?"

First of all, you do NOT have to tell your friends. But you might be stressing about opening up and having everyone know your business. No worries! Therapists have to keep everything you share with them on the down-low. That's the law. So, when you chat with your therapist, you can be sure your secrets are safe and won't be spread around.

The Endgame...For Now

You've watched Isa and Jeremy navigate their way to the conclusion that they're ready to stop letting SAD negatively affect their lives. So now you have the chance to do just that. SAD can feel overwhelming, but with the tools and techniques outlined in this book, you have the power to take control and rewrite your story.

It's like being handed a map to navigate through the wilderness, or a compass to guide you through a storm. You have the ability to rewire your brain, calm your body, embrace the suck, and cultivate good habits that will help you manage your symptoms and live a more fulfilling life. The journey may be tough at times, but the reward is priceless.

Need a confidence boost? **Here's a recap of all the information and skills you have in your toolbelt now:**

Chapter 1: Why Do I Feel This Way?

Back in the day, humans developed a "fight, flight, or freeze" mechanism in our brains to protect us from predators, but now it's causing some of us to freak out unnecessarily in social situations—that's the short explanation of anxiety disorders.

Social Anxiety Disorder (SAD) is a fear of social situations that can really cramp our style and affect our friendships, school performance, and overall happiness.

Unlike shyness, social anxiety is persistent and can really mess with our daily lives. SAD causes us to experience negative thoughts, which lead to negative feelings, which lead to behaviors that convince our brains that our thoughts were rightfully negative in the first place! The good news is that there are ways to manage it.

Break any one of those links in the chain of SAD (thoughts, feelings, behavior) and you can break the cycle.

Chapter 2: Reprogram Your Brain

Your thoughts are the source of the cycle of anxiety. Your brain is impressionable, and it believes anything you tell it. **Cognitive behavioral therapy (CBT)** helps you break the negative thought loops perpetuated by the cycle of anxiety. Through CBT, you can learn to identify and challenge negative thoughts and beliefs, which can decrease anxiety over time. It's like magic, *but for your mind.*

Noticing the thought allows you to identify thinking errors. Once an error is identified, you can challenge it and adopt a different and more realistic thought even if it doesn't seem believable. Your brain will believe whatever you tell it, so keep feeding your brain positive thoughts, and over time it will believe you!

Chapter 3: Calm Your Body

When the brain "believes" it's in danger, it will give you symptoms as if you actually were in real danger—even when you're not. It's an impressive defense mechanism (thanks, ancestors), but it's a false alarm. This link can be broken by convincing your brain that you're not in actual danger.

How do you do that? By proving to the brain that you're safe and calming your body through **breathing, grounding, visualization**, and **progressive**

muscle relaxation. Once your body is calm, your brain will say, "Oh, we're calm; I guess there's no danger after all!"

Chapter 4: Embrace The Suck

Avoiding uncomfortable situations seems natural, but when it comes to SAD, it actually makes things worse. When you avoid something and go to great lengths to get out of an uncomfortable situation, your brain thinks, "We worked so hard to get out of this—this must be dangerous," and it will record this situation as such. The next time you encounter the same situation, your brain says, "Nope, not doing that again," and it keeps going on until the thought moves from being "uncomfortable" to "unbearable."

This feedback loop is the most powerful link in the cycle of anxiety, and tackling this is the hardest yet most effective way to take out SAD from the root. So how do you break the chain? By building a **fear ladder**, doing little exposure challenges, and staying consistent. Your brain is watching, so the more you do it, the more it will realize, "Ah, it's not as bad as I thought!"

Now the negative thoughts start to disappear. And no negative thought equals no anxiety! Fascinating, right?

Chapter 5: The Significant Six

As the wise old saying goes, you are the sum of your habits. And since your body and mind go together, you need to have good habits when it comes to self-care. That's where the **six significant habits** come in: sleep, diet, exercise, acts of kindness, journaling, and mindfulness.

Do you believe in science? Then you better believe that these habits can significantly improve your happiness and well-being. Remember, you don't need to overwhelm yourself by changing every little detail about your daily life right now. Even making small improvements to your daily habits can help manage the symptoms of SAD over time.

Chapter 6: Your Quest For Support

Dealing with social anxiety can be really tough and scary—especially when it comes to talking to others about it. But opening up is the first step to feeling better. Your parents, guidance counselors, and family friends are there to support you, so tell them when you're ready to seek therapy.

Therapists are trained pros with loads of knowledge and experience. It's guaranteed they will understand you in a way that others don't. This is because they have dedicated their lives to helping others with similar issues. Just as you trust a driving instructor to teach you driving or a math tutor to improve your algebra skills, you can trust a therapist's competency to help you manage your anxiety and live a healthier life. All you have to do is start, be patient, and trust the process!

Thank You!

I hope that this book has brought you laughter, inspiration, and a fresh perspective. You are the heroes of your own stories, and I'm grateful to have played a small part in helping you navigate the challenges of SAD.

Remember, you are capable of incredible things. Embrace your uniqueness, face your fears, and never stop believing in yourself. We believe in you, and we're cheering you on at every step of the way.

As you close this book, take the lessons and insights you've gained and carry them with you into the world. Trust your instincts, be kind to yourself and others, and always remember that you have the power to take back control of your life.

Useful Resources

Apps

1. **Apps focused on Anxiety management:**
   - **Mindshift**—Offers a range of useful functions including strategies and tips for anxiety management, coping cards, meditation exercises, belief experiments, fear ladder and exposure therapy (iOS: https://apps.apple.com/us/app/mindshift-cbt-anxiety-relief/id634684825) (Android: https://play.google.com/store/apps/details?id=com.bstro.MindShift&hl=en&gl=US)
   - **Sanvello**—Helps manage stress, anxiety or depression using mindfulness and cognitive behavioral therapy (CBT) skills. It includes a community to connect with others (https://www.sanvello.com/)
   - **Woebot**—Interactive chatbot to help challenge negative thinking patterns (https://woebothealth.com/)
   - **Worry Watch**—Helps to identify and analyze worries, journaling, and tracking anxiety (https://shorturl.at/syBFY)

2. **Apps focused on mindfulness and meditation:**
   - Calm (https://www.calm.com/)
   - Headspace (https://www.headspace.com/)
   - SmilingMind (https://www.smilingmind.com.au/)
   - Breathwrk (https://www.breathwrk.com/)

Websites with educational resources:
- The National Institute for Mental Health (https://www.nimh.nih.gov/)
- The Association for Behavioural and Cognitive Therapy (www.abct.org)
- The Child Mind Institute (https://childmind.org/)
- Anxiety Canada (www.anxietycanada.com)
- The Anxiety Disorders Association of America (www.adaa.org)
- Head to Health (https://www.headtohealth.gov.au/)

YouTube Channels dedicated to mental health:
- Kati Morton (https://www.youtube.com/@Katimorton)
- Anxiety Canada (https://www.youtube.com/@AnxietyCanada)
- Psych To Go (https://www.youtube.com/@Psych2go)
- Natasha Daniels (https://www.youtube.com/@Natashadanielsocdtherapist)
- ADAA Anxiety (https://www.youtube.com/@ADAA_Anxiety)

Podcasts:
- *Social Anxiety Solutions by Sebastiaan van der Schrier (https://open.spotify.com/show/1HnWEk7drUleJQAISj049K)*
- *Social Anxiety Remedy by Parker Dunham (https://open.spotify.com/show/7fxTH5HGWLXtAoSALwrgVb)*
- *Your Social Anxiety Bestie podcast with Sadie by Sadie Hall (https://open.spotify.com/show/1QlfWFzvAYS96vjy7blaRE)*
- *On Our Minds with Ashley and Tayler by Student Reporting Labs (https://open.spotify.com/show/2ETfXzY5C033g9yO1I2t7Q)*
- *She persisted by Sadie Sutton (https://open.spotify.com/show/53JGhfgwgD92PjNTpBukzH)*

Books:
- **The Anxiety Workbook for Teens:** Activities to Help You Deal with Anxiety and Worry. By Lisa M. Schab, LCSW (https://shorturl.at/deuCT)

- **Anxiety relief for Teens:** Essential CBT Skills and Mindfulness Practices to Overcome Anxiety and Stress. By Regine Galanti, PhD (https://shorturl.at/ivyGQ)
- **The Shyness and Social Anxiety Workbook for Teens:** CBT and ACT Skills to Help you Build Social Confidence. By Jennifer Shannon, LMFT (https://shorturl.at/MPQSW)
- **My Anxious Mind:** A Teen's Guide to Managing Anxiety and Panic. By Michael A. Tompkins, PhD, Katherine Martinez and Michael Sloan (https://shorturl.at/mtMP2)

Online Support Communities:
- **Hey Peers** (Heypeers.com)
- **7 Cups** (https://www.7cups.com/)
- **The Tribe Wellness Community** (https://support.therapytribe.com/)
- **ADAA's Online Peer-to-Peer Communities** (https://adaa.org/find-help/support)

For emergencies:
- **Teen Line:** call 800-852-8336 or check out (https://www.teenline.org/): For immediate support and a teen-to teen conversation and strategies to cope with anxiety.
- **National Alliance on Mental Illness (NAMI) Helpline:** call 1-800-950-NAMI (6264): Get questions answered on mental health issues and get free information and referrals to programs, educational resources, support groups etc.
- **National Suicide Prevention Lifeline:** call 1-800-273-TALK (8255): If your anxiety is causing you to have suicidal thoughts, please call this free hotline immediately.
- **If you're based outside of the U.S, but need immediate help:** Go to: (https://checkpointorg.com/global/), find the relevant number according to your location and call immediately.

References

1. Almlöv, J., Carlbring, P., Källqvist, K., Paxling, B., Cuijpers P., & Andersson, G. (2011) *Therapist effects in guided internet-delivered CBT for anxiety disorders. Behav Cogn Psychother*, M39(3), 311–22. https://doi: 10.1017/S135246581000069X Epub 2010, Dec. 13.
2. Amir, N., Beard, C., Taylor, C. T., Klumpp, H., Elias, J., Burns, M., & Chen, X. (2009) *Attention training in individuals with generalized social phobia: A randomized controlled trial. J Consult Clin Psychol*, 77(5), 961–973. https://doi: 10.1037/a0016685
3. Alden, L. E., & Taylor, C. T. (2004) Interpersonal processes in social phobia. *Clin Psychol Rev*, 24(7), 857–882. https://doi: 10.1016/j.cpr.2004.07.006. PMID: 15501559.
4. Bögels, S. M., Van Oosten, A., Muris, P., & Smulders, D. (2001). Familial correlates of social anxiety in children and adolescents. *Behaviour Research and Therapy*, 39(3), 273–287. https://doi.org/10.1016/S0005-7967(00)00005-X
5. Blakemore, S. (2008). The social brain in adolescence. *Nature Reviews Neuroscience*, 9(4), 267–277. https://doi.org/10.1038/nrn2353
6. Caouette, J. D., & Guyer, A. E. (2014). Gaining insight into adolescent vulnerability for social anxiety from developmental cognitive neuroscience. *Developmental Cognitive Neuroscience*, 8, 65–76. https://doi.org/10.1016/j.dcn.2013.10.003
7. Collins, A. (2021). *How to socialise when you have social anxiety.* https://www.opencolleges.edu.au/blog/2016/07/04/mhm-socialise-social-anxiety/

8. Garcia-Lopez, L. J., Olivares, J., Beidel, D., Albano, A. M., Turner, S., & Rosa, A. (2006). *Efficacy of three treatment protocols for adolescents with social anxiety disorder: A 5-year follow-up assessment. J Anxiety Disord, 20*(2),175–91. https://www.sciencedirect.com/science/article/abs/pii/S0887618505000253

9. Haller, S. P. W., Cohen Kadosh, K., Scerif, G., & Lau, J. Y. F. (2015). Social anxiety disorder in adolescence: How developmental cognitive neuroscience findings may shape understanding and interventions for psychopathology. *Developmental Cognitive Neuroscience, 13,* 11–20. https://doi.org/10.1016/j.dcn.2015.02.002

10. Heimberg, R. G., Brozovich, F. A., & Rapee, R. M. (2010). A cognitive-behavioral model of social anxiety disorder: Update and extension. In S. G. Hofmann & P. M. DiBartolo (Eds.), *Social anxiety: Clinical, developmental, and social perspectives,* 2, (pp. 395–422). Academic Press.

11. Hirsch C. R., Clark, D. M., Mathews, A., & Williams, R. (2003). *Self-images play a causal role in social phobia. Behav Res Ther, 41*(8), 909–921. https://doi: 10.1016/s0005-7967(02)00103-1 PMID: 12880646.

12. Kerns, C. M., Read, K. L., Klugman, J., & Kendall, P.C. (2013). *Cognitive behavioral therapy for youth with social anxiety: Differential short and long-term treatment outcomes. J Anxiety Disord, 27*(2), 210–215. https://doi: 10.1016/j.janxdis.2013.01.009 Epub 2013, Feb 15.

13. Kessler, R. C. (2017). *National Comorbidity Survey: Adolescent Supplement* (NCS-A) 2001-2004. Inter-university Consortium for Political and Social Research. https://doi.org/10.3886/ICPSR28581.v6

14. Knappe, S., Beesdo, K., Fehm, L. et al. (2009). Associations of familial risk factors with social fears and social phobia: *Evidence for the continuum hypothesis in social anxiety disorder.* J Neural Transm 116, 639–648. https://doi.org/10.1007/s00702-008-0118-4

15. Leigh, E., & Clark D. M. (2018) *Understanding social anxiety disorder in adolescents and improving treatment outcomes: Applying the cognitive model of Clark and Wells* (1995). Clin Child Fam Psychol Rev, 21(3), 388–414. https://doi: 10.1007/s10567-018-0258-5

16. Leichsenring, F., Salzer, S., Beutel, M. E., Herpertz, S., Hiller, W., Hoyer, J., et al. (2013). Psychodynamic therapy and cognitive-behavioral therapy in social anxiety disorder: A multicenter randomized controlled trial. *American Journal of Psychiatry, 170*(7), 759–767. https://doi.org/10.1176/appi.ajp.2013.12081125

17. McEvoy, P. M., & Perini, S.J. (2009). *Cognitive behavioral group therapy for social phobia with or without attention training: A controlled trial. 23*(4), 519-528. https://doi: 10.1016/j.janxdis.2008.10.008 Epub 2008 Oct 28.

18. Melfsen, S., Kühnemund, M., Schwieger, J., Warnke, A., Stadler, C., Poustka, F., & Stangier, U. (2011). Cognitive behavioral therapy of socially phobic children focusing on cognition: A randomised wait-list control study. *Child Adolesc Psychiatry Ment Health. 5*(1), 5. https://doi: 10.1186/1753-2000-5-5

19. American Psychiatric Association. (2013). *Diagnostic and statistical manual of mental disorders* (5th ed.). American Psychiatric Association.

20. Mayo Clinic. (2023). *Social anxiety disorder* (social phobia). https://www.mayoclinic.org/diseases-conditions/social-anxiety-disorder/symptoms-causes/syc-20353561

21. *Social Anxiety Disorder: Recognition, Assessment and Treatment. (2013).* National Collaborating Centre for Mental Health (UK). Available from: https://www.ncbi.nlm.nih.gov/books/NBK327674/

22. *Social Anxiety Disorder* (n.d.) National Institute of Mental Health (NIMH) https://www.nimh.gov/health/statistics/social-anxiety-disorder